Activities
for a
Differentiated
Classroom

Developed by

Wendy Conklin, M.A.

SHELL EDUCATION

Consultant

Chandra C. Prough, M.S.Ed.
National Board Certified
Newport-Mesa
Unified School District

Contributing Authors

Scarlett Mikeska
Tracy Rieger

Publishing Credits

Dona Herweck Rice, *Editor-in-Chief*; Lee Aucoin, *Creative Director*; Don Tran, *Print Production Manager*; Timothy J. Bradley, *Illustration Manager*; Chris McIntyre, M.A.Ed., *Editorial Director*; Sara Johnson, M.S.Ed., *Senior Editor*; Aubrie Nielsen, M.S., *Associate Education Editor*; Robin Erickson, *Interior Layout Designer*; Juan Chavolla, *Production Artist*; Ana Clark, *Illustrator*; Stephanie Reid, *Photo Editor*; Corinne Burton, M.S.Ed., *Publisher*

Shell Education
5301 Oceanus Drive
Huntington Beach, CA 92649-1030
http://www.shelleducation.com
ISBN 978-1-4258-0735-1
© 2011 by Shell Educational Publishing, Inc.
Reprinted 2012

Table of Contents

Understanding Differentiation

As I conduct workshops with teachers of all ages and grade levels, I hear a familiar tune: *Differentiating curriculum is worrisome and stressful.* I believe this is due to the fact that teachers do not know how to begin differentiating. Their administrators tell them that they must differentiate, but teachers are overwhelmed with the task of doing it because there is not a clear explanation of what to do. Teachers know the theory. They know they need to do it. They just do not know *how* to do it.

The right way to differentiate depends on the unique students in a classroom. To successfully differentiate, teachers must first know their students. Knowing what academic level students are at helps us understand where to begin. When we have students who do not succeed, we find out why they are not succeeding. Then, we look for the type of support that they need to help them learn specific concepts. We make adjustments when students have trouble comprehending material. We look for new ways to present information, new manipulatives that make sense, and opportunities to provide additional support. As our struggling students grow, we can then scaffold the amount of support that we provide so that students continue to grow instead of leaning too heavily on that support. Differentiation is about meeting the needs of *all* students and providing the right amount of challenge for *all* students.

What Should I Differentiate and Why?

Many teachers have heard the terms *content*, *process*, and *product* when it comes to differentiating curriculum, but few have the time to ponder how these words apply to what they do in their classrooms. Below is a chart that briefly defines how we differentiate and why we differentiate.

Differentiating Curriculum

How	Why
Vary the Content (what is taught)	**Readiness** (students are not at the same academic level)
Vary the Process (how it is taught)	**Learning Styles** (students prefer different ways of learning)
Vary the Product (what students produce)	**Interests** (students have different passions)

Differentiation Strategies in This Book

What Differentiation Strategies Can I Use?

Each book in the *Activities for a Differentiated Classroom* series introduces a selection of differentiation strategies. Each lesson in this book uses one of the six differentiation strategies outlined below. The strategies are used across different curriculum areas and topics to provide you with multiple real-world examples.

Differentiation Strategy		Lessons in This Book
	Tiered Assignments	• Nonfiction Text—*Language Arts* • Place Value—*Math* • Creature Features—*Science* • Cultural Connections—*Social Studies*
K	**Kaplan's Depth and Complexity**	• Fairy Tales—*Language Arts* • Rounding and Estimation—*Math* • Who Swallowed Whom?—*Science* • Important Inventions—*Social Studies*
	Menu of Options	• Plot—*Language Arts* • Playing with Fractions—*Math* • Blast Off to Space—*Science* • Citizenship—*Social Studies*
	Leveled Learning Centers	• Life Stories: Biographies and Autobiographies—*Language Arts* • Symmetry—*Math* • States of Matter—*Science* • Local Government—*Social Studies*
	Discovery Learning	• Persuasive Writing—*Language Arts* • Finding Perimeter—*Math* • Forces of Motion—*Science* • Exploring Entrepreneurship—*Social Studies*
Contract	**Leveled Learning Contracts**	• Poetry Skills—*Language Arts* • Multiplication Strategies—*Math* • Earth's Shifting Surface—*Science* • Making Maps—*Social Studies*

Differentiation Strategies in This Book *(cont.)*

Tiered Assignments

One way to ensure that all students in a classroom advance—using the same skills and ideas regardless of readiness levels—is to tier lessons. Often referred to as *scaffolding*, tiered assignments offer multilevel activities based on key skills at differing levels of complexity. One example of this is leveled reading texts. All students can learn about the Civil War by reading texts that are leveled according to the different reading abilities in the classroom. You can also provide comprehension questions that are leveled. Each student comes away with essential grade-appropriate skills in addition to being sufficiently challenged. The entire class works toward one goal (learning about the Civil War), but the path to that goal depends on each student's readiness level.

So, how do you tier lessons?

- **Pick the skill, concept, or strategy that needs to be learned.** For example, a key concept would be using reading skills and strategies to understand and interpret a variety of informational texts.

- **Think of an activity that teaches this skill, concept, or strategy.** For this example, you could have students summarize the information and include a main idea in the summary.

- **Assess students.** You may already have a good idea of your students' readiness levels, but you can further assess them through classroom discussions, quizzes, tests, or journal entries. These assessments can tell you if students are above grade level, on grade level, or below grade level.

- **Take another look at the activity you developed.** How complex is it? Where would it fit on a continuum scale? Is it appropriate for above-grade-level learners, on-grade-level learners, below-grade-level learners, or English language learners?

- **Modify the activity to meet the needs of the other learners in the class.** Try to get help from the specialists in your school for English language learners, special education students, and gifted learners. For this example, summarizing with a main idea would be appropriate for on-grade-level students. Above-grade-level students should include supporting details in their summaries. The below-grade-level students will need a few examples provided for their summaries. English language learners will begin with the same examples given to below-grade-level students so that they understand what is expected of them. Then, they will summarize information verbally to you.

Remember, just because students are above grade level does not mean that they should be given more work. And, just because students are below grade level does not mean that they should be given less work. Tiered lessons are differentiated by varying the *complexity*, not necessarily the *quantity* of work required for the assignment. Likewise, all tiered activities should be interesting and engaging.

Differentiation Strategies in This Book (cont.)

Kaplan's Depth and Complexity

By differentiating the curriculum using depth and complexity, curricular expectations are defined clearly, and students are able to stay more focused by asking questions to increase their knowledge. Sandra Kaplan (2001) describes eight categories of depth and three categories of complexity that teachers can use to guide students to greater understanding.

Depth

Language of the Disciplines (vocabulary)—This refers to learning the specific, specialized, and technological terms associated with a particular area of study or discipline.

Details (parts, variables)—This refers to the learning of the specific attributes, traits, and characteristics that describe a concept, theory, principle, and even a fact.

Patterns (repetition, predictability)—This refers to recurring events represented by details.

Trends (courses of action, directions)—This refers to the factors that influence events.

Unanswered Questions (missing parts, unclear ideas)—This refers to the ambiguities and gaps of information recognized within an area or discipline of study.

Rules (order, structure)—This refers to the natural or human-made structure or order of things that explains the phenomena within an area or discipline of study.

Ethics (judging, opinions)—This refers to the dilemmas or controversial issues that complicate an area or study of discipline.

Big Ideas (principles, generalizations)—This refers to the generalizations, principles, and theories that distinguish themselves from the facts and concepts of the area or discipline of study.

Complexity

Over Time (relationships between past, present, and future)—This refers to the understanding of time as an agent of change and recognition that the passage of time changes our knowledge of things.

Points of View (multiple perspectives, opposing viewpoints)—This refers to the concept that there are different perspectives and that these perspectives affect the way ideas and objects are viewed and valued.

Interdisciplinary Connections (relationships between and across disciplines)—This refers to both integrated and interdisciplinary links in the curriculum. Interdisciplinary connections can be made within, between, and among various areas or study of disciplines.

Differentiation Strategies in This Book (cont.)

Menu of Options

Providing students the opportunity to choose what activity they want to do increases their level of interest in what they are doing or learning. However, many students do not often get the chance to make choices about their work. It can be challenging and time-consuming for teachers to develop a variety of engaging activities. Yet offering options is essential to getting students interested and motivated in learning. When students are involved in something of their own choosing, they are more engaged in the learning process (Bess 1997; Brandt 1998).

Choices in the classroom can be offered in a variety of ways. Students can choose what they will learn (content), how they will learn (process), and how they will show what they have learned (product). A menu of options is a strategy that differentiates product by giving students the opportunity to choose from a list of highly engaging activities.

The menu of options strategy works well for many reasons. First, it operates much like a menu from a restaurant. A person looking at a menu sees all the choices. Some cost more and some cost less. No one likes going to a restaurant and being told what to eat. People enjoy choosing what they prefer from the menu. In the same way, a menu of options offers students many different projects from which to choose. These projects are assigned various point values. The point values depend on the amount of work or detail involved in the project. Students must earn a set number of points determined by the teacher, but they can choose which activities they want to complete. Any kind of point system can be used. For example, basic projects that do not take much time can be worth 10 points. Projects that take a moderate amount of time and energy can be worth 30 points. Projects that are very time-consuming can be worth 50 points. If the students need to complete 80 points total, they can get to that total number in many different ways. They may choose a 50-point project and a 30-point project. Or, they may choose two 30-point projects and two 10-point projects.

Secondly, a menu of options is effective because the freedom of choice allows students to complete projects that are of interest to them. This increases the chance that the students will produce high-quality products. Students like to feel in control. When given a list to choose from, students often choose projects that they like or that fit their learning styles. If the teacher provides enough variety, then all students can find projects that they feel passionate about.

As an alternative to creating a menu of options based on point systems, a teacher can create three or four sections on a menu of options and ask students to choose one project from each section. This strategy is helpful when there are a particular set of concepts that the teacher needs to be sure that students have learned.

Differentiation Strategies in This Book (cont.)

Leveled Learning Centers

Providing academically appropriate assignments for students is important. All students need to be sufficiently challenged so that they can continue to increase their knowledge. If assignments are too easy, students will be bored and they will not learn anything new. If assignments are too difficult, students will experience stress, which can also deter the learning process.

Leveling, or tiering, assignments will ensure that all students work on parallel tasks designed to have varied levels of depth, complexity, and abstractness along with differing degrees of scaffolding, support, and direction depending on each student and the topic. All students work toward one goal, concept, or outcome, but the lesson is tiered to allow for different levels of readiness and performance. As students work, they build on their prior knowledge and understanding. Tiered assignments are productive because all students work on similar tasks that provide individual challenges. Students are motivated to be successful according to their own readiness levels as well as their own learning preferences.

When possible, teachers should also look for ways to offer students choices. When students are given a chance to choose their activities, they are likely to be more engaged in the learning process (Bess 1997; Brandt 1998).

Leveled learning centers combine the best of both worlds—choices and tiered assignments. Leveled learning centers are centers with activities that are leveled according to academic difficulty. Each student is given a choice to work at any of the centers. The following are some best practices for using leveled learning centers:

- There should be at least three centers to choose from.
- Within each center, there are activities that are appropriate for below-grade-level students, on-grade-level students, and above-grade-level students.
- The varying activity levels can be indicated by different shapes:
    - △ above-grade-level activities can be identified with a triangle
    - ☐ on-grade-level activities can be identified with a square
    - ◯ below-grade-level activities can be identified with a circle
    - ☆ activities for English language learners can be identified with a star. These activities should contain vocabulary and language support. Partner English language learners with students who are proficient in English for additional support.

Using leveled learning centers also provides busy teachers with unique opportunities for assessment. As students work in their centers, teachers can observe students and document their progress using checklists. Teachers will be able to identify students who need more challenging activities or scaffolded work, and assignments can be quickly adjusted.

Discovery Learning

Discovery learning is an inquiry-based learning method in which a teacher sets up an experiment, acts as a coach, and supports students in the process of discovering solutions.

Discovery learning is largely attributed to Jerome Bruner. During the 1960s and 1970s, Bruner worked with the National Science Foundation to develop science curriculum. Bruner believed science curriculum should help students to become problem solvers by using discovery and inquiry. As students test hypotheses and develop generalizations, they interact with the environment around them and discover solutions. When they discover their own solutions, they will better remember what was taught (Bruner 2004).

Bruner thought that science was more than merely the accumulation of wisdom from textbooks. He believed knowing was a process. When students are given structured problems, they learn concepts and problem-solving skills. The desire for knowledge motivates students to solve problems. Bruner's theory of instruction consists of the four principles below.

Curiosity and Uncertainty

The first principle of Bruner's theory is that teachers should offer experiences to make students want to learn or be predisposed to learning. The problem to be explored must offer alternative solutions. This experience must have an amount of uncertainty, which in turn would pique students' curiosity and interest in solving the problem.

Structure of Knowledge

Bruner's (2004) second (and some say most important) principle states that the teacher "must specify the ways that a body of knowledge should be structured so that it can be most readily grasped" by students. He believed that teachers could present any problem to students as long as it was simplified so students could understand it. To do this, the problem must be represented by either enactive representation (a set of actions), iconic representation (a set of pictures), or symbolic representation (logical statements).

Sequencing

Bruner's third principle states that the learner should be led sequentially through content. This will help students to understand and transfer the knowledge that is learned. First, students should complete hands-on activities that are concrete. Next, they should have a visual representation of the concept. Finally, students should move to using vocabulary or symbols having to do with the concept.

Motivation

Bruner's final principle is that rewards from the teacher should gradually decrease until students are wholly satisfied with their intrinsic abilities to solve problems. It is important for teachers to provide feedback so that students can develop confidence in their understanding.

Differentiation Strategies in This Book (cont.)

Leveled Learning Contracts

Leveled learning contracts are individualized, independent agreements between the teacher and students. Leveled learning contracts provide structure to students while at the same time allowing them to think critically and work on complex ideas at their own readiness levels. They encourage students to develop independence and time-management skills (Winebrenner 1992). Often teachers set up leveled learning contracts so that students have the opportunity to select from a list of choices. Leveled learning contracts are also flexible. Teachers can use leveled learning contracts in the everyday classroom with all students. Topics can be the same or varied, but the way students learn and show what they have learned can differ according to abilities, learning styles, and readiness levels. Leveled learning contracts can also be used for remedial help. This gives students the necessary time to spend on topics that are confusing at first. Leveled learning contracts can be used as enrichment options. This will provide some students the opportunity to delve deeper into topics and spend extra time on a class topic. Or, the contracts can be used for acceleration if the school district is committed to continually providing accelerated curriculum to students who need it.

After determining the assignments and projects that the learning contracts should contain, meet with students individually or in small groups to explain the contracts. It is the teacher's responsibility to set up each contract so that students will learn the needed skills. These skills should be listed on the contract along with the ways in which students will apply those skills. Students, however, take on the responsibility for their own learning. The contract must be signed by both the student and the teacher. Some teachers also choose to use learning contracts in order to allow advanced students to contract out of whole-class lessons. If above-grade-level students already know the content, you can write a learning contract with them to give them focused tasks related to the curriculum. They can then complete the learning contract instead of participating in lessons based on content that they already know (Winebrenner 1992).

It is also helpful if an assessment and a rubric are included with the leveled learning contracts. A rubric will help students to know how they will be evaluated on their contract projects. Grades can be broken down into a few different categories. One grade might be based on the student's work ethic. Did he or she follow the rules on the contracts? Did he or she work toward goals? Another grade is based on the actual assignments. Select one or two assignments and check them for accuracy, quality, and completion. The last grade could be based on an assessment. Allow students to complete self-assessments as well as peer assessments on one or two assignments.

As a final note, teachers should set up periodic appointments with students to check their progress. Teachers might also have students work with partners or groups to monitor one another's daily progress. This will allow time for teachers to work with small groups or individual students who are having trouble.

Grouping Students

What Grouping Strategies Can I Use?

There are many variables that a teacher must consider when grouping students to create a successful learning environment. These variables include gender, chemistry between students, social maturity, academic readiness, and special needs. Some students will work well together while others will have great difficulty.

In this book, for ease of understanding, readiness levels are represented with a shape (triangle for above-grade level, square for on-grade level, and circle for below-grade level). In a classroom, however, a teacher might want to change the names for leveled groups from time to time. A teacher might use colors, animal names, or athletic team names to group students. For example, a teacher could cut out and distribute three different colors of construction paper squares, with each color representing a different readiness level. The teacher would tell all the "yellow square" students to find partners who also have a yellow square. This way, the teacher creates homogeneous groups while also allowing students to choose partners.

The following grouping strategies demonstrate various ways to group students in a differentiated classroom. This section is included so that you can learn to quickly group your students and easily apply the strategies.

Flexible Grouping

Flexible grouping means that members of a group change frequently. Routinely using the same grouping technique can lead to negative feelings, feelings of shame or a stigma associated with some group levels, lack of appropriate instruction, boredom, and behavior problems in the classroom. Flexible grouping can change the classroom environment daily, making it more interesting. It takes away the negative feelings and stigma of the struggling students because groups are always changing. No longer are the struggling students always in the same group.

Flexible grouping can occur within one lesson or over an entire unit. Try to modify groups from day to day, week to week, and unit to unit. Flexible grouping can include partner work, cooperative grouping, and whole-class grouping. Students' academic levels, interests, social chemistry, gender, or special needs can determine their placement in a particular group. Organize charts like the ones on the following pages to help you keep track of how you are grouping your students.

Grouping Students *(cont.)*

What Grouping Strategies Can I Use? *(cont.)*

Homogeneous Grouping

Homogeneous grouping brings together students who have the same readiness levels. It makes sense to group students homogeneously for reading groups and for language and mathematics skills lessons. To form groups, assess students' readiness levels in a content area. Then, order students from highest to lowest in readiness, and place them in order on a three-row horizontal grid.

One way to create homogeneous groups is by using the chart below. Notice that students in the same row have similar readiness levels.

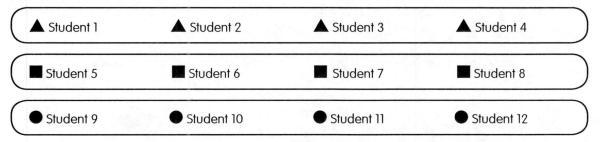

Homogeneous groups share similar readiness levels.

Heterogeneous Grouping

Heterogeneous grouping combines students with varied academic readiness levels. When grouping heterogeneously, look for some diversity in readiness and achievement levels so students can support one another as they learn together.

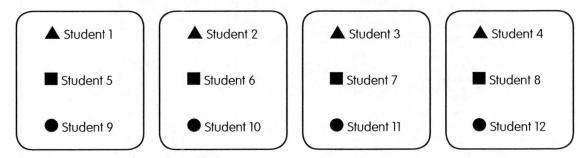

Heterogeneous groups have varying readiness levels.

Another strategy for heterogeneous grouping is to group by interest. Interest groups combine students with varied levels of achievement to create groups that have common interests. Other strategies for heterogeneous grouping include allowing students to self-select their groups, grouping by locality of seating arrangements in the classroom, and selecting groups at random.

Grouping Students (cont.)

What Grouping Strategies Can I Use? (cont.)

Flexogeneous Grouping

Flexogeneous grouping allows for the flexible grouping of homogeneous and heterogeneous groups within the same lesson. Students switch groups at least one time during the lesson to create another group. For example, the homogeneous groups meet for half the lesson and then switch to form heterogeneous groups for the rest of the lesson.

One easy flexogeneous grouping strategy is to jigsaw or mix up already established homogeneous groups. To jigsaw groups, allow homogeneous groups of students to work together for part of the lesson (circle, square, and triangle groups). Then, distinguish group members by labeling them *A*, *B*, and *C* within the same group. All the *A*s form a new group, the *B*s form a new group, and the *C*s form a new group.

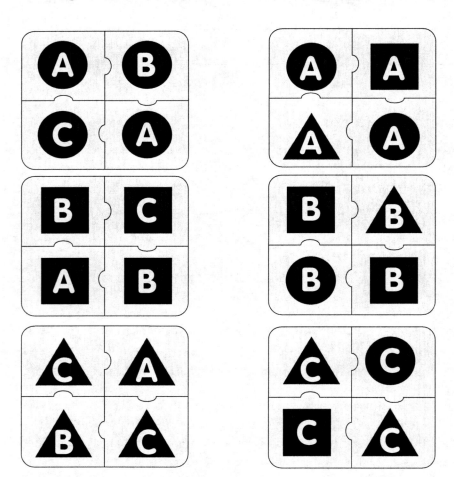

Flexogeneous grouping uses homogeneous and heterogeneous groups in a single lesson.

Working with English Language Learners

Strategies for Working with English Language Learners

Use visual media as an alternative to written responses. Have all students express their thinking through visual media, such as drawings, posters, or slide shows. This is an effective strategy for eliciting responses from English language learners. This also fosters creativity in all students, challenges above-grade-level students, provides opportunities for artistically inclined students who may struggle academically, and avoids singling out English language learners.

Frame questions to make the language accessible. At times, you will need to rephrase questions to clarify meaning for English language learners. Framing questions makes the language accessible to all students. Higher-order questions can be asked without reducing their rigor. Pose questions for English language learners with question stems or frames.

Example Question Stems/Frames

- What would happen if…?
- What is your opinion?
- Why do you think…?
- How would you prove…?
- Would it be better if…?

- How is _____ related to _____?
- If you could _____, what would you do?
- Can you invent _____?
- Why is _____ important?
- Why is _____ better than _____?

Give context to questions to enable understanding. This can be done by placing pictures or small icons directly next to key words. English language learners also benefit from chunking sentences. For example, with the question *In the ocean, how do wind and ocean currents make boats move?* English language learners can see right away that the question is about the ocean, so they have a context for answering the question.

Provide English language learners with sentence stems or frames to encourage higher-order thinking. These learners need language tools to help them express what they think. Sentence stems or frames will not only get the information you need and want from your English language learners, but it will also model how they should be speaking. You can provide these sentence stems or frames on small sticky notes for students to keep at their desks, or write them on laminated cards and distribute them to students when necessary.

Example Sentence Stems/Frames

- This is important because…
- This is better because…
- This is similar because…
- This is different because…

- I agree with _____ because…
- I disagree with _____ because…
- I think _____ because…
- I think _____ will happen because…

Partner up, and let partners share aloud. Have English language learners work with language-proficient students to answer questions, solve problems, or create projects. Language-proficient partners can provide the academic vocabulary needed to express ideas. Prepare your language-proficient students to work with language learners by explaining that they must speak slowly and clearly and give these learners time to think and speak.

Working with English Language Learners *(cont.)*

How Can I Support English Language Learners?

All teachers should know the language-acquisition level of each of their English language learners. Knowing these levels will help to plan instruction. Using visuals to support oral and written language for students at Level 1 will help make the language more comprehensible. Students at Levels 2 and 3 benefit from pair work in speaking tasks, but they will need additional individual support during writing and reading tasks. Students at Levels 4 and 5 may still struggle with comprehending the academic language used during instruction, as well as with reading and writing. Use the chart below to plan appropriate questions and activities.

Proficiency Levels for English Language Learners—Quick Glance

Proficiency Level	Questions to Ask	Activities/Actions		
Level 1—Entering • minimal comprehension • no verbal production	• Where is…? • What is the main idea? • What examples do you see? • What are the parts of…? • What would happen if…? • What is your opinion?	• listen • point	• draw • circle	• mime
Level 2—Beginning • limited comprehension • short spoken phrases	• Can you list three…? • What facts or ideas show…? • What do the facts mean? • How is _____ related to _____? • Can you invent…? • Would it be better if…?	• move • match	• select • choose	• act/act out
Level 3—Developing • increased comprehension • simple sentences	• How did _____ happen? • Which is your best answer? • What questions would you ask about…? • Why do you think…? • If you could _____ , what would you do? • How would you prove…?	• name • label • tell/say	• list • categorize	• respond (with 1–2 words) • group
Level 4—Expanding • very good comprehension • some errors in speech	• How would you show…? • How would you summarize…? • What would result if…? • What is the relationship between…? • What is an alternative to…? • Why is this important?	• recall • compare/contrast • describe	• retell • explain • role-play	• define • summarize • restate
Level 5—Bridging • comprehension comparable to native English speakers • speaks using complex sentences	• How would you describe…? • What is meant by…? • How would you use…? • What ideas justify…? • What is an original way to show…? • Why is it better that…?	• analyze • evaluate • create	• defend • justify • express	• complete • support

How to Use This Book

Teacher Lesson Plans

Each lesson is presented in a straightforward, step-by-step format so that teachers can easily implement it right away.

Differentiation Strategies are highlighted for quick reference.

Standards are aligned to grade-level content and English language learner needs.

Materials lists outline items needed for each lesson. If lessons call for slide show software, you might use *Microsoft Powerpoint®* or *Prezi®*. Additional resources are listed on page 167.

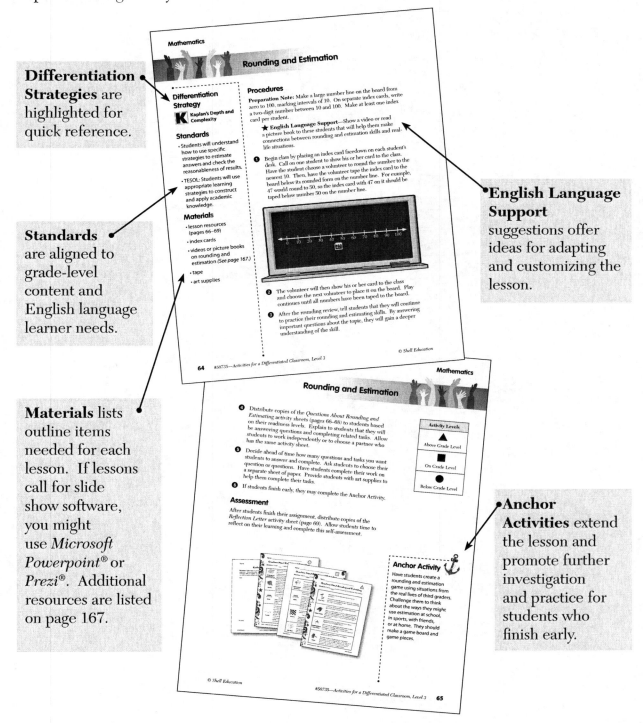

English Language Support suggestions offer ideas for adapting and customizing the lesson.

Anchor Activities extend the lesson and promote further investigation and practice for students who finish early.

How to Use This Book (cont.)

Lesson Resources

These pages include student reproducibles and teacher resources needed to implement each lesson.

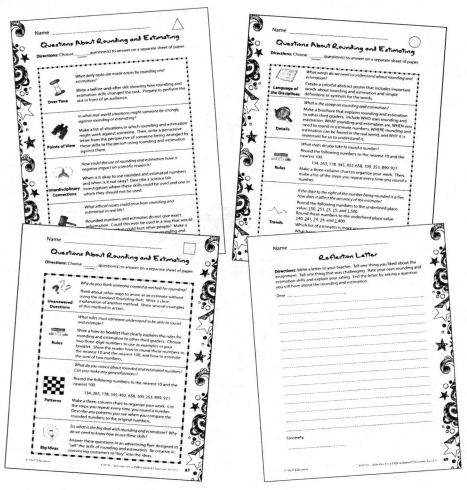

Teacher Resource CD

Helpful reproducibles and images are provided on the accompanying CD. Find a detailed listing of the CD contents on page 168.

- Reproducible PDFs of all student activity sheets and teacher resource pages
- Reproducible PDFs of blank graphic organizers
- Answer key

Correlations to Standards

Shell Education is committed to producing educational materials that are research and standards based. In this effort, we have correlated all of our products to the academic standards of all 50 states, the District of Columbia, and the Department of Defense Dependent Schools.

How to Find Standards Correlations

To print a customized correlation report of this product for your state, visit our website at **http://www.shelleducation.com** and follow the on-screen directions. If you require assistance in printing correlation reports, please contact Customer Service at 1-877-777-3450.

Purpose and Intent of Standards

The No Child Left Behind (NCLB) legislation mandates that all states adopt academic standards that identify the skills students will learn in kindergarten through grade 12. While many states had already adopted academic standards prior to NCLB, the legislation set requirements to ensure the standards were detailed and comprehensive.

Standards are designed to focus instruction and guide adoption of curricula. Standards are statements that describe the criteria necessary for students to meet specific academic goals. They define the knowledge, skills, and content students should acquire at each level. Standards are also used to develop standardized tests to evaluate students' academic progress.

Teachers are required to demonstrate how their lessons meet state standards. State standards are used in the development of all of our products, so educators can be assured that they meet the academic requirements of each state.

McREL Compendium

We use the Mid-continent Research for Education and Learning (McREL) Compendium to create standards correlations. Each year, McREL analyzes state standards and revises the compendium. By following this procedure, McREL is able to produce a general compilation of national standards. Each lesson in this product is based on one or more McREL standards. The chart on page 20 lists each standard taught in this book and the page numbers for the corresponding lessons.

TESOL Standards

The lessons in this book promote English language development for English language learners. The standards listed on page 21, from the Teachers of English to Speakers of Other Languages (TESOL) Association, support the language objectives presented throughout the lessons.

Correlations to Standards *(cont.)*

	McREL Standards	Lesson Title	Page
Language Arts	1.6, Level II: Students will use strategies to write for a variety of purposes.	Persuasive Writing	34
	6.2, Level II: Students will know the defining characteristics of a variety of literary forms and genres.	Fairy Tales	22
		Nonfiction Text	28
		Life Stories: Biographies and Autobiographies	46
	6.3, Level II: Students will understand the basic concept of plot.	Plot	40
	6.7, Level II: Students will understand the ways in which language is used in literary texts.	Poetry Skills	52
Mathematics	2.4, Level II: Students will understand the meaning of place value in numbers.	Place Value	58
	2.5, Level II: Students will understand that symmetry is a basic property of a figure and be able to recognize and identify lines of symmetry.	Symmetry	88
	3.4, Level II: Students will understand how to use specific strategies to estimate answers and check the reasonableness of results.	Rounding and Estimation	64
	3.6, Level II: Students will understand the effect of multiplication on the size and order of numbers.	Multiplication Strategies	70
	4.1, Level II: Students will understand the basic measures of perimeter, area, volume, capacity, mass, angle, and circumference.	Finding Perimeter	82
	5.2, Level II: Students will understand the concept of fractions and be able to identify and name fractional parts.	Playing with Fractions	76
Science	2.1, Level II: Students will understand how the features on Earth's surface are constantly changed by a combination of forces and processes.	Earth's Shifting Surface	106
	3.2, Level II: Students will understand that Earth is one of several planets that orbit the sun, and the moon orbits Earth.	Blast Off to Space	112
	4.1, Level II: Students will understand that many characteristics of animals are inherited from its parents, and other characteristics are learned.	Creature Features	118
	6.4, Level II: Students will understand how changes in the environment have different effects on organisms.	Who Swallowed Whom?	124
	8.1, Level II: Students will understand that matter has different states, all matter has distinct properties, and some materials can change from one state to another through heating and cooling.	States of Matter	94
	10.6, Level II: Students will understand the relationship between the strength of a force and its effect on an object.	Forces of Motion	100
Social Studies	Civics 1.6, Level II: Students will understand the major things that governments do in one's school, community, state, and nation.	Local Government	136
	Civics 10.1, Level II: Students will understand the importance of volunteerism as a characteristic of American society.	Citizenship	160
	Economics 1.5, Level II: Students will understand that entrepreneurs are people who use resources to produce innovative goods and services they hope people will buy.	Exploring Entrepreneurship	130
	Geography 1.1, Level II: Students will understand the basic elements of maps and globes.	Making Maps	148
	History 3.1, Level II: Students will understand that technologies often have costs as well as benefits and can have an enormous effect on people and other living things.	Important Inventions	142
	History 7.3, Level II: Students will understand various aspects of family life, structures, and roles in different cultures and in many eras.	Cultural Connections	154

Correlations to Standards (cont.)

	TESOL Standards	Lesson Title	Page
TESOL 2.1	Students will use English to interact in the classroom.	Persuasive Writing	34
		Finding Perimeter	82
		Forces of Motion	100
		Exploring Entrepreneurship	130
		Making Maps	148
TESOL 2.2	Students will use English to obtain, process, construct, and provide subject matter information in spoken and written form to achieve academically in all content areas.	Fairy Tales	22
		Nonfiction Text	28
		Life Stories: Biographies and Autobiographies	46
		Poetry Skills	52
		Multiplication Strategies	70
		Earth's Shifting Surface	106
		Blast Off to Space	112
		Cultural Connections	154
		Citizenship	160
TESOL 2.3	Students will use appropriate learning strategies to construct and apply academic knowledge.	Plot	40
		Place Value	58
		Rounding and Estimation	64
		Playing with Fractions	76
		Symmetry	88
		States of Matter	94
		Creature Features	118
		Who Swallowed Whom?	124
		Local Government	136
		Important Inventions	142

Language Arts

Fairy Tales

Differentiation Strategy

 Kaplan's Depth and Complexity

Standards

- Students will know the defining characteristics of a variety of literary forms and genres.

- TESOL: Students will use English to obtain, process, construct, and provide subject matter information in spoken and written form to achieve academically in all content areas.

Materials

- lesson resources (pages 24–27)

- a selection of fairy tales (See page 167.)

- index cards

- chart paper and markers

Procedures

Preparation Note: Before class begins, prepare a Fairy Tale Word Wall in the classroom. Make sure students can reach it.

1 Read aloud a fairy tale to students. Ask students to think about the elements that make this story a fairy tale.

2 Introduce the defining characteristics of fairy tales to the whole class.

- The defining characteristics are usually *magic*, *items in numbers of three or seven*, and *characters that are animals or royalty*.

- There is usually a *good character* and an *evil character*.

- The setting is often a *castle*, a *forest*, or a *village*.

- Fairy tales usually have *problems that get solved* by the end of the stories.

- Fairy tales usually begin with *"Once upon a time"* and end with *"happily ever after."*

3 Read aloud a second fairy tale. Distribute copies of the *Is It a Fairy Tale?* activity sheet (page 24) to students and display a copy for the class. Ask the class to identify the characteristics of fairy tales that are present in the second fairy tale.

4 Distribute copies of the *Fairy Tale Fun* activity sheets (pages 25–27) to students based on their readiness levels.

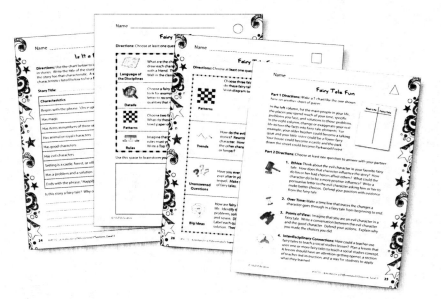

Fairy Tales

5 Pair students with partners at the same readiness level. Explain to students that they will work together to answer at least one of the questions on the activity sheet.

★ **English Language Support**—Make sure English language learners are partnered with language-proficient students at their readiness levels. Explain some strategies for working with English language learners to their partners. For example, ask students to read the activity sheets aloud slowly and clearly. Have them point to the text as they read. Explain that it is acceptable for English language learners to draw their responses or to give them verbally.

6 Ask students to read each question carefully and discuss it with their partners. Then, have them select at least one question to complete together. During this time, meet with students who are working below grade level and with English language learners. If necessary, read the directions and questions aloud to them. Provide examples of the activities and clarify the directions.

7 When most pairs have completed the activity sheets, allow time for volunteers to share their finished products with peers.

8 If students finish early, they may complete the Anchor Activity.

Assessment

Informally assess student learning by observing students as they work with their partners. Review student responses to the leveled questions to gain a clearer understanding of their knowledge about fairy tales.

Activity Levels
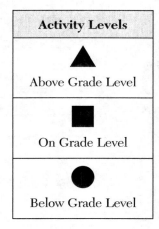
Above Grade Level
On Grade Level
Below Grade Level

Anchor Activity

Have students outline or brainstorm a *fractured fairy tale* based on a fairy tale that they enjoy. A fractured fairy tale changes the characters, setting, point of view, or plot of a familiar fairy tale. What would students change about the story? Whose perspective would they show? Let students share their brainstormed ideas or outline with the class.

Name _____

Is It a Fairy Tale?

Directions: Use the chart below to identify the characteristics of fairy tales in stories. Write the title of the story. Place a checkmark (✔) in the box if the story has that characteristic. A story will typically have at least six of the characteristics listed below to be a fairy tale.

Story Title: _____

Characteristics	Checkmark (✔)
Begins with the phrase, "*Once upon a time . . .*"	
Has magic	
Has items in numbers of three or seven	
Has animal or royal characters	
Has good characters	
Has evil characters	
Setting is a castle, forest, or village	
Has a problem and a solution	
Ends with the phrase, "*Happily ever after.*"	

Is this story a fairy tale? Why or why not?

_____

_____

_____

_____

Name _____

Fairy Tale Fun

Part 1 Directions: Make a T-chart like the one shown here on another sheet of paper:

In the left column, list the main people in your life, the places you spend much of your time, specific problems you face, and solutions to those problems. In the right column, change or exaggerate your real life to turn the facts into fairy-tale elements. For example, your older brother could become a talking goat and your little sister could be a flower fairy. Your house could become a castle and the park down the street could become Parkwood Forest.

Part 2 Directions: Choose at least one question to answer with your partner.

1. **Ethics:** Think about the evil character in your favorite fairy tale. How does that character influence the story? How do his or her bad choices affect others? What could the character do to be a more positive influence? Write a persuasive letter to the evil character asking him or her to make better choices. Defend your position with evidence from the fairy tale.

2. **Over Time:** Make a time line that traces the changes a character goes through in a fairy tale from beginning to end.

3. **Points of View:** Imagine that you are an evil character in a fairy tale. Write a conversation between the evil character and the good character. Defend your actions. Explain why you made the choices you did.

4. **Interdisciplinary Connections:** How could a teacher use fairy tales to teach a social studies lesson? Plan a lesson that uses one or more fairy tales to teach a social studies concept. A lesson should have an attention-getting opener, a section of teacher-led instruction, and a way for students to apply what they learned.

Name _____

Fairy Tale Fun

Directions: Choose at least one question to answer with your partner.

Patterns

Choose three fairy tales. Read these on your own. What do these fairy tales have in common? Create a three-ring Venn diagram to compare and contrast these tales.

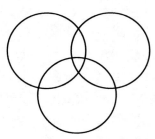

Trends

How do the evil characters in fairy tales change the stories? Rewrite a famous fairy tale without the evil character. How would the story be different? How would the other characters behave? Would the story be shorter or longer?

Unanswered Questions

Have you ever wondered what happened after the *happily ever after* in your favorite fairy tale? Write a fairy tale sequel. Make sure to use at least six of the characteristics of fairy tales.

Big Ideas

How are fairy tales similar to real life? Think about your life. Identify the good characters, the evil characters, problems, solutions, magic, and items in numbers of three and seven. Divide a sheet of paper into four quadrants. Label each quadrant *main characters*, *setting*, *problem*, and *solution*. Then, plan a fairy tale based on your own life.

Name _____

Fairy Tale Fun

Directions: Choose at least one question to answer with your partner.

Language of the Disciplines

What are the characteristics of a fairy tale? On index cards, draw each characteristic and label it. Share your cards with a friend. Then, put your cards on the Fairy Tale Word Wall in the classroom.

Details

Choose a fairy tale to read with your partner. As you read, look for examples of fairy-tale characteristics. Write a letter to recommend the story to classmates. Explain the qualities that make it a great fairy tale.

Patterns

Choose two fairy tales. Read them with your partner. What do these stories have in common? Make a list on lined paper of the things that the stories have in common.

Rules

Imagine that your friend wants to write a fairy tale. What rules must your friend follow to make it a real fairy tale? Write a Top Ten list of rules for your friend.

Use this space to brainstorm your ideas.

Nonfiction Text

Differentiation Strategy

 Tiered Assignments

Standards

- Students will know the defining characteristics of a variety of literary forms and genres.

- TESOL: Students will use English to obtain, process, construct, and provide subject matter information in spoken and written form to achieve academically in all content areas.

Materials

- lesson resources (pages 30–33)

- sentence strips or index cards

- bucket, container, or box

- a variety of nonfiction texts (*See page 167.*)

- sticky notes

- chart paper and markers

Procedures

❶ Begin the lesson with a "word splash" activity. Before class begins, write the following terms on sentence strips or index cards.

boldface	*caption*	*chart*	*glossary*
graph	*heading*	*index*	*italics*
key word	*picture*	*photograph*	*sidebar*
subheading	*table of contents*	*title*	

❷ Place the sentence strips in a bucket, container, or box. Carry the bucket to the front of the classroom and pretend to trip. Spill the sentence strips so that they "splash" across the floor.

❸ Ask students to organize the words into categories that make sense to them. Have students explain the categories that they chose. Then, lead students in a discussion about what the words mean and where each text feature is found in nonfiction texts.

❹ Tell students that good readers look at *and* read nonfiction texts. Using all the features provided helps readers better understand the content. Explain to students that you want them to become experts at recognizing these nonfiction text features. To do this, they will go on a Feature Hunt.

❺ Place students in small heterogeneous groups for the Feature Hunt. Provide students with a wide variety of nonfiction texts, such as textbooks, how-to books, manuals, game directions, cookbooks, encyclopedias, and newspapers. Give students time to explore the materials. Distribute sticky notes to each group. Ask students to look through the nonfiction texts and place sticky notes on examples of text features. The goal of this Feature Hunt is for groups to find the most examples of different nonfiction text features.

❻ Distribute a large piece of chart paper to each group. Have students write the names of the text features that they found and a brief description of the text that they read. Invite a few groups to share their lists. Wrap up the activity by discussing as a class the importance of text features.

Nonfiction Text

❼ Next, ask students to look at your selection of nonfiction books and to choose a topic to research independently.

★ **English Language Support**—Provide research materials for students at their independent reading levels. Another option is to pair these students with reading buddies or classroom volunteers who can read the texts aloud and point out key facts.

❽ Distribute copies of the *Using Nonfiction Text Features* activity sheets (pages 30–32) to students based on their readiness levels. Allow students time to use your books and answer the questions on their activity sheets.

Activity Levels
▲
Above Grade Level
■
On Grade Level
●
Below Grade Level

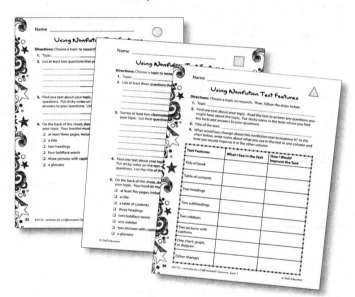

❾ If students finish early, they may complete the Anchor Activity.

Assessment

Use the *Nonfiction Text Features Scoring Guide* (page 33) to assess students' work. There is a separate scoring guide for each leveled activity sheet.

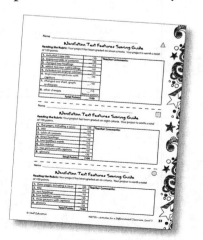

Anchor Activity

Have students give star ratings and short recommendations for the nonfiction texts that are on your shelves or in the library. Just like professionals make recommendations, have these students write their opinions on index cards to hang underneath the location of the texts.

Name _____

Using Nonfiction Text Features

Directions: Choose a topic to research. Then, follow the steps below.

1. Topic: _____

2. Find one text about your topic. Read the text to answer any questions you
   might have about the topic. Put sticky notes in the texts where you find
   key facts and answers to your questions.

3. Title of the text: _____

4. What would you change about this nonfiction text to improve it? In the
   chart below, write notes about what you see in the text in one column and
   how you would improve it in the other column.

Text Features	What I See in the Text	How I Would Improve the Text
Title of book		
Table of contents		
Two headings		
Two subheadings		
Two sidebars		
Two pictures with captions		
One chart, graph, or diagram		
Other changes		

Name _____

Using Nonfiction Text Features

Directions: Choose a topic to research. Then, follow the steps below.

1. Topic: _____

2. List at least three questions that you have about your topic.

   _____

   _____

   _____

   _____

3. Survey at least two classmates to find out what they want to know about your topic. List their questions.

   _____

   _____

   _____

   _____

   _____

   _____

4. Find one text about your topic. Read the text to answer your questions. Put sticky notes on the text where you find key facts and answers to your questions. List the title of the text: _____

   _____

5. On the back of this sheet, sketch your ideas for a nonfiction booklet about your topic. Your booklet must have:

   ❏ at least five pages, including a cover

   ❏ a title

   ❏ a table of contents

   ❏ three headings

   ❏ two boldface words

   ❏ one sidebar

   ❏ two pictures with captions

   ❏ a glossary

Name _____

Using Nonfiction Text Features

Directions: Choose a topic to research. Then, follow the steps below.

1. Topic: _____

2. List at least two questions that you have about your topic.

   _____

   _____

   _____

   _____

   _____

3. Find one text about your topic. Read the text to answer your two questions. Put sticky notes on the text where you find key facts and answers to your questions. List the title of your text:

   _____

   _____

4. On the back of this sheet, sketch your ideas for a nonfiction booklet about your topic. Your booklet must have:

   ❑ at least three pages, including a cover

   ❑ a title

   ❑ two headings

   ❑ four boldface words

   ❑ three pictures with captions

   ❑ a glossary

Name _____

Nonfiction Text Features Scoring Guide

Reading the Rubric: Your project has been graded on seven criteria. Your project is worth a total of 100 points.

		Teacher Comments:
1. included a new title	__ /10	
2. improved table of contents	__ /20	
3. changed two headings	__ /10	
4. added two new subheadings	__ /10	
5. included two original sidebars	__ /20	
6. improved two pictures with captions	__ /20	
7. changed one chart, graph, or diagram	__ /10	
8. other changes	__ /10 bonus points!	
Total Points	__ /100	

— —

Name _____

Nonfiction Text Features Scoring Guide

Reading the Rubric: Your project has been graded on eight criteria. Your project is worth a total of 100 points.

		Teacher Comments:
1. five pages, including a cover	__ /20	
2. title	__ /10	
3. table of contents	__ /10	
4. three headings	__ /10	
5. two boldface words	__ /10	
6. one sidebar	__ /10	
7. two pictures with captions	__ /10	
8. glossary	__ /20	
Total Points	__ /100	

— —

Name _____

Nonfiction Text Features Scoring Guide

Reading the Rubric: Your project has been graded on six criteria. Your project is worth a total of 100 points.

		Teacher Comments:
1. three pages, including a cover	__ /20	
2. title	__ /10	
3. two headings	__ /10	
4. four boldface words	__ /20	
5. three pictures with captions	__ /20	
6. glossary	__ /20	
Total Points	__ /100	

Persuasive Writing

Differentiation Strategy

 Discovery Learning

Standards

- Students will use strategies to write for a variety of purposes.
- TESOL: Students will use English to interact in the classroom.

Materials

- lesson resources (pages 36–39)
- chart paper and markers
- art supplies
- ballots and ballot box
- *Vote for Class Mayor* banner (optional)
- patriotic decorations (optional)

Procedures

Preparation Note: If you wish, before class begins, decorate the classroom with patriotic banners, streamers, and flags. Make a large banner that says *Vote for Class Mayor*. Hang the banner in a central location in the classroom.

1 Explain to students that the class needs a mayor. Ask students to describe the job of a mayor, using their background knowledge. Clarify and correct details as needed. Tell students that the class mayor will do some of the same things a town mayor does.

2 Distribute copies of the *Vote for Me Discovery Learning Challenge* activity sheet (page 36) to students. Read the challenge aloud as students follow along.

3 As a class, discuss the character traits a class mayor should possess. List the traits on chart paper. For example, a class mayor should be honest, trustworthy, well-spoken, friendly, and responsible.

4 Encourage all students to run for the position of class mayor. However, explain that those who choose not to run will serve as campaign managers for the candidates. Ideally, about half the students will be candidates and half will be partnered with them as their campaign managers.

★ **English Language Support**—Encourage these students to run for class mayor. Whether they choose to run for the position or be a campaign manager, partner them with language-proficient students to complete the project.

5 Distribute copies of the *Vote for Me Campaign Plan* activity sheet (page 37) to candidate-manager teams. Give students time to complete the plan. Students will create a campaign slogan, a poster, and a persuasive speech. Provide students with paper and various art supplies. Circulate and assist as needed, but be careful not to direct students what to do.

Persuasive Writing

6 Give candidates time to rehearse their campaign speeches. Encourage campaign managers to critique their candidates' speeches to help to improve them prior to the election rally. Ask campaign managers to prepare a three-sentence introduction of their candidate. The introduction should clearly state the candidate's name, strengths and skills, and plans for the future.

7 Hold an election rally in which candidates display their posters and present their speeches to the class. Make sure that each candidate's name is clearly displayed in the classroom. The campaign managers should introduce their candidates.

8 Immediately after the speeches, distribute blank ballots to students. Collect the ballots in a ballot box. Count the ballots and announce the winner of the election.

9 If students finish their campaign preparation early, they may complete the Anchor Activity.

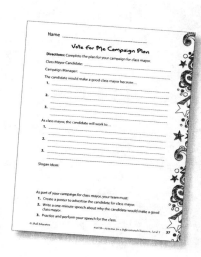

Assessment

Use the *Vote for Me Skills Checklist* (page 38) to document observations about students' work. Once the election is over, ask students what they discovered about elections. What worked best? What did not work as well as they had hoped? Was it hard to run a campaign? What persuaded public opinion most? What did the winner do differently? Distribute copies of the *Vote for Me Campaign Reflection* activity sheet (page 39) to students to complete as a self-assessment.

Anchor Activity

Have students think of something at school that they would like to change. Have them write a persuasive letter to the principal in which they explain their position on the issue. They should provide suggestions to address the issue or solve the problem.

Name _____

Vote for Me Discovery Learning Challenge

The Challenge: Our class needs a leader. This leader will represent our class within the school community. This leader will also act as a spokesperson for the teacher. This leader will help the class work on important school issues. You, the students of our class, will vote for this leader in an election. This leader will be the class mayor.

Think:

What traits should a class mayor have?

_____

_____

What would you need to do to get elected class mayor?

_____

_____

What are some ways political candidates tell voters about themselves?

_____

_____

_____

Plan:

If you choose to become a candidate for class mayor, you must:

1. Invent a catchy campaign slogan.
2. Think of reasons why you would make a great leader.
3. Plan some things you would like to do for your class as class mayor.
4. Create a campaign poster.
5. Give a persuasive speech in front of your class.

Choose: Would you like to run for class mayor or be a campaign manager for a candidate for mayor? _____

Use the back of this sheet to brainstorm your campaign for class mayor.

Name _____

Vote for Me Campaign Plan

Directions: Complete the plan for your campaign for class mayor.

Class Mayor Candidate: _____

Campaign Manager: _____

The candidate would make a good class mayor because…

1. _____

_____

2. _____

_____

3. _____

_____

As class mayor, the candidate will work to…

1. _____

_____

2. _____

_____

3. _____

_____

Slogan ideas:

As part of your campaign for class mayor, your team must:

1. Create a poster to advertise the candidate for class mayor.

2. Write a one-minute speech about why the candidate would make a good class mayor.

3. Practice and perform your speech for the class.

Vote for Me Skills Checklist

Teacher Directions: Use the checklist below to assess students' performance. Use checkmarks (✔) in the criteria columns to indicate proficiency.

Student Name	Works cooperatively	Stays on task	Uses persuasive writing techniques	Provides effective feedback to peers	Contributes good ideas

Name _____

Vote for Me Campaign Reflection

Candidate: _____

Campaign Manager: _____

Illustrate your most memorable moment of the campaign or election.

```

```

Caption: _____

_____

What do you think was the best thing about your campaign? Explain your opinion.

_____

_____

How would you change your campaign?

_____

_____

Rate yourself using the numbers 1 to 5.

　　　1 = Always　2 = Usually　3 = Sometimes　4 = Not really　5 = Not at all

_____ I did my absolute best work on this campaign!

_____ I was a good team player.

_____ I worked hard to come up with a catchy slogan and new ideas.

_____ I was a respectful listener for my classmates.

_____ In front of an audience, I spoke clearly and made eye contact.

Plot

Differentiation Strategy

   ☑ **Menu of Options**

Standards

- Students will understand the basic concept of plot.
- TESOL: Students will use appropriate learning strategies to construct and apply academic knowledge.

Materials

- lesson resources (pages 42–45)
- leveled picture books (See page 167.)
- chart paper and markers
- audio recorder

Procedures

1 Begin the lesson with a picture-book read-aloud. Choose any age-appropriate picture book that has a problem, a conflict, and a resolution. After reading, ask students to identify story elements. Sketch a simple graphic organizer on chart paper to help students organize their ideas. Be sure to include the title, the author's name, the main characters, the setting, the main events, the conflict, and the resolution.

2 Next, sketch a simple "roller-coaster" graphic organizer to chart the story's plot development. Ask volunteers to mark the main events, the conflict, and the resolution on the roller-coaster plotline.

3 Next, place students in homogeneous groups of three. Give each group a picture book at the appropriate readiness level. Have the groups read the picture books and record the story elements on graphic organizers like the one completed in Step 2.

4 Ask groups to summarize their stories for the class, using ideas from their graphic organizers. Make sure students are able to correctly identify the story's plot. Correct any misconceptions and clarify the concepts at this time.

5 Distribute copies of the *Plot Menu of Options* activity sheets (pages 42–43). Explain to students that they will choose activities from the menu to learn more about plot. Review the options as a class and answer any questions that students may have. Ask students to use a chapter book that they are currently reading or have recently read to complete the activities. Decide how many points students need to complete from the menu of options, and set a due date for the projects.

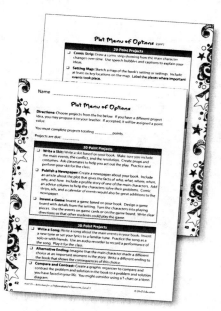

Plot

6 Next, have students use the *Plot Action Plan* activity sheet (page 44) to plan their activities.

★ **English Language Support**—Use this time to meet with these students to make sure that they choose projects at their readiness levels. Reread the activity directions and show students some sample projects so they may understand what is expected. If necessary, modify the activities to meet individual needs. Help students to complete their action plans.

7 If students finish early, they may complete the Anchor Activity.

Assessment

Give students time to complete their activities from the menu of options. Assess students' work using the *Plot Project Rubric* (page 45).

Anchor Activity

Have students outline their own idea for a story, but have them leave out a key part (such as the conflict). How would this affect the story? Students can also analyze other stories that they enjoy in the same way. What would removing key features do to the story?

Name _____

Plot Menu of Options

Directions: Choose projects from the list below. If you have a different project idea, you may propose it to your teacher. If accepted, it will be assigned a point value.

You must complete projects totaling _____ points.

Projects are due: _____

50-Point Projects
❑ **Write a Skit:** Write a skit based on your book. Make sure you include the main events, the conflict, and the resolution. Create props and costumes. Ask classmates to help you act out the play. Practice and perform your skit for the class.
❑ **Publish a Newspaper:** Create a newspaper about your book. Include an article about the plot that gives the facts of *who, what, where, when, why*, and *how*. Include a profile story of one of the main characters. Add an advice column to help the characters solve their problems. Comic strips, ads, and a calendar of events would also be great additions to the newspaper.
❑ **Invent a Game:** Invent a game based on your book. Design a game board with details from the setting. Turn the characters into playing pieces. Use the events on game cards or on the game board. Write clear directions so that other students could play the game.

30-Point Projects
❑ **Write a Song:** Write a song about the main events in your book. Invent a new tune or set your lyrics to a familiar tune. Practice the song as a solo or with friends. Use an audio recorder to record a performance of the song. Play it for the class.
❑ **Alternative Ending:** Imagine that the main character made a different choice at an important moment in the story. Write a different ending to the book that shows the consequences of this choice.
❑ **Compare and Contrast:** Create a graphic organizer to compare and contrast the problem and solution in the book to a problem and solution you have faced in your life. You might consider using a T-chart or a Venn diagram.

Plot Menu of Options *(cont.)*

20-Point Projects

❏ **Comic Strip:** Draw a comic strip showing how the main character changes over time. Use speech bubbles and captions to explain your ideas.

❏ **Setting Map:** Sketch a map of the book's setting or settings. Include at least six key locations on the map. Label the places where important events took place.

❏ **Write a Letter:** Pretend you are a character in the book. Write a letter to another character in the book. Mention some of the people, places, and events from the story.

❏ **Make a Dictionary:** Make a mini-dictionary that gives the definitions of the terms *plot, conflict, resolution,* and *cause and effect.* Draw picture examples from your book to illustrate the terms.

10-Point Projects

❏ **Conflict and Resolution:** Fold a piece of paper in half. On one half, draw and label a picture of the story's conflict. On the other half, draw and label a picture of the story's resolution.

❏ **Time Line:** Make a time line of at least five important events in your book.

❏ **Venn Diagram:** Create a Venn diagram to compare the main problem in the story to the main problem in another story you have recently read.

❏ **Character Web:** Make a character web showing as many traits as you can about the main character in your book.

❏ **Journal Entry:** Write a journal entry from the future that tells about how the main character's life turned out.

Extra Credit Projects

❏ _____

_____

_____

_____

Name _____

Plot Action Plan

Directions: Complete the action plan below to help organize your projects.

You must complete projects totaling _____ points.

Projects are due: _____

Project Name	Points	Steps to Take

Total Points: _____

Plot Project Rubric

Teacher Directions: Use this rubric to assess students' plot projects. Give the bottom half to students so that they may complete a self-evaluation.

Student Name:		
Project Description	**Points Possible**	**Points Earned**
Total Points:		

Teacher Comments: _____

_____

_____

- -

Plot Project Rubric Self-Assessment

Directions: Use this rubric to assess your plot projects.

Student Name:		
Project Description	**Points Possible**	**Points Earned**
Total Points:		

Student Comments: _____

_____

_____

Life Stories: Biographies and Autobiographies

Differentiation Strategy

Leveled Learning Centers

Standards

- Students will know the defining characteristics of a variety of literary forms and genres.

- TESOL: Students will use English to obtain, process, construct, and provide subject matter information in spoken and written form.

Materials

- lesson resources (pages 48–51)
- index cards
- craft sticks

Procedures

Preparation Note: Set up five learning centers in the classroom, each with enough space for three to six students. Each center will have activities for different readiness levels. Cut apart copies of the *Life Stories Centers* activity sheets (pages 48–49) and place them at each learning center, along with the corresponding *Table Talk Questions* (page 50). Also, stock the centers with lined paper, index cards, and pencils.

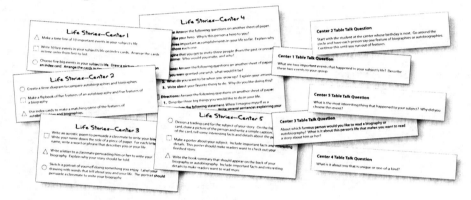

❶ Explain to students that they will be able to explore five learning centers at which they will begin writing either their autobiography or a biography about another classmate.

❷ Before working in the centers, students must choose to write either an autobiography or a biography about a classmate. Once they have decided, they should write five interview questions to ask their subjects. If they plan to write an autobiography, they should still write five questions to answer about themselves. These questions will provide students with the details that they will need to complete the center activities.

❸ Have students conduct their interviews or answer their questions. Remind students that it is important to accurately record their subjects' answers to the interview questions. Give students some note-taking tips, such as using abbreviations and symbols, and writing sentence fragments instead of complete sentences.

Life Stories: Biographies and Autobiographies

④ Have craft sticks labeled with triangles, squares, and circles. Distribute the triangle sticks to above-grade-levels students. Distribute square sticks to on-grade-level students. Distribute circle sticks to below-grade-level students. Explain that students should choose center activities that match the shape on their craft sticks.

⑤ Give students time to explore the centers. Allow students to choose their own starting points in the rotation. The only limitation is that they must choose a center with an available seat or workspace. Ask students to carefully read the directions. Teach students the "ask three, then me" rule. When following this rule, students must ask three classmates for help before asking the teacher for help. This encourages independence during center activities.

⑥ After students have read the directions, have them discuss the *Table Talk Questions* activity sheet (page 50) posted at the center. These questions are designed to prepare students for the activity.

★ **English Language Support**—Pair English language learners with English-proficient students to serve as their guides during center activities. Ask these guides to read directions aloud and answer questions. Encourage the guides to show their work to English language learners as examples.

⑦ If students finish early, they may complete the Anchor Activity.

Assessment

Ask questions of students to assess their understanding as they work at the centers. Use the *Life Stories Center Activities Checklist* (page 51) to document this assessment.

Activity Levels
Above Grade Level
On Grade Level
Below Grade Level

Anchor Activity
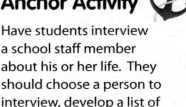

Have students interview a school staff member about his or her life. They should choose a person to interview, develop a list of questions, and schedule an appointment with the staff member. Students can then turn the information into a biography poster to hang in a school hallway so that all students can get to know the staff better.

Life Stories—Center 1

△ Make a time line of 10 important events in your subject's life.

☐ Write 10 key events in your subject's life on index cards. Arrange the cards in time order from first to last.

○ Choose five big events in your subject's life. Draw a picture of each one on an index card. Arrange the cards in time order from first to last.

- -

Life Stories—Center 2

○ Create a Venn diagram to compare autobiographies and biographies.

☐ Make a flipbook of five features of an autobiography and five features of a biography.

△ Use index cards to make a matching game of the features of autobiographies and biographies.

- -

Life Stories—Center 3

☐ Write an acrostic poem to persuade a classmate to write your biography. Write your name down the side of a piece of paper. For each letter in your name, write a word or phrase that describes you or your life.

△ Write a letter to a classmate persuading him or her to write your biography. Explain why your story should be told.

○ Sketch a portrait of yourself doing something you enjoy. Label your drawing with words that tell about you and your life. The portrait should persuade a classmate to write your biography.

Life Stories—Center 4

△ **Directions:** Answer the following questions on another sheet of paper.

1. Describe your hero. Why is this person a hero to you?

2. List three important accomplishments in your life so far. Explain why you chose each one.

3. Imagine that you get to invite three people (from the past or present) to dinner. Who would you invite, and why?

○ **Directions:** Answer the following questions on another sheet of paper.

1. If you were granted one wish, what would it be?

2. What do you want to be when you grow up? Explain your answer.

3. Write about your favorite thing to do. Why do you like doing this?

▢ **Directions:** Answer the following questions on another sheet of paper.

1. Describe three big things you would like to do in your life.

2. Complete the following statement: When I imagine myself as a grown-up, I see _____. Write several sentences explaining your statement.

3. What makes you special? Make a list of five things that make you unique.

- -

Life Stories—Center 5

○ Design a trading card for the subject of your story. On the front of the card, draw a picture of the person and write a simple caption. On the back of the card, tell some interesting facts and details about the person.

▢ Make a poster about your subject. Include important facts and interesting details. This poster should make readers want to check out your finished story.

△ Write the book summary that should appear on the back of your biography or autobiography. Include important facts and interesting details to make readers want to read more.

Table Talk Questions

Directions: Cut apart the question strips. Post the strips at the correct learning centers.

- -

Center 1 Table Talk Question

What are two important events that happened in your subject's life? Describe these two events to your group.

- -

Center 2 Table Talk Question

Start with the student at the center whose birthday is next. Go around the circle and have each person say one feature of biographies or autobiographies. Continue this until you run out of features.

- -

Center 3 Table Talk Question

About which famous person would you like to read a biography or autobiography? What is it about this person's life that makes you want to read a story about him or her?

- -

Center 4 Table Talk Question

What is it about you that is unique or one-of-a-kind?

- -

Center 5 Table Talk Question

What is the most interesting thing that happened to your subject? Why did you choose this event?

Life Stories Center Activities Checklist

Teacher Directions: Use the checklist below to assess students' performance. Use checkmarks (✔) in the criteria columns to indicate proficiency.

Student Name	Follows directions	Stays on task	Contributes to discussions	Completes work on time

Poetry Skills

Differentiation Strategy

Leveled Learning Contracts

Standards

- Students will understand the ways in which language is used in literary texts.

- TESOL: Students will use English to obtain, process, construct, and provide subject matter information in spoken and written form.

Materials

- lesson resources (pages 54–57)

- dictionaries

- poster board

- samples of completed poetry projects

- variety of poetry books (See page 167.)

- art supplies

- old newspapers

- magazines

- catalogs

Procedures

1 Ask students to choose partners for a poetry activity. Distribute copies of the *Poetry Skills Vocabulary* activity sheet (page 54) to students. Assign each student pair a different word on the activity sheet. Explain that they are responsible for researching the definition in a dictionary and finding examples to share with the class. Ask each pair to make a simple poster to display the information.

2 Give each pair of students time to share their vocabulary poster with the class and to teach the meaning of their term. After each presentation, have students add the new word, definition, and examples to their charts. Students should keep their charts to use as a reference throughout the lesson.

3 Next, distribute copies of the *Poetry Skills Learning Contract* activity sheet (pages 55–57) to students based on their readiness levels. Ask students to review the contract options and choose three activities to complete independently.

★ **English Language Support**—Read aloud the project choices to these students. Help them choose projects appropriate to their abilities. Provide examples of completed poetry projects to clarify expectations. If necessary, partner them with English proficient students to complete the activities.

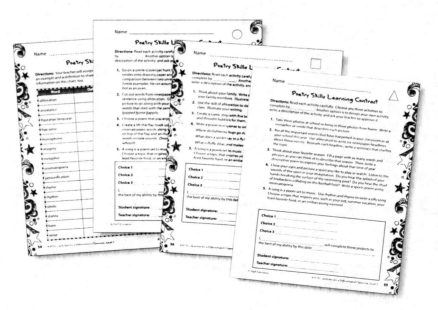

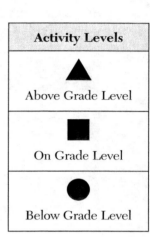

Poetry Skills

4 Have students sign their contracts. Meet with students individually to review their selections, clarify directions, and sign their contracts.

5 Allow your above-grade-level and on-grade-level students to work independently on their contract activities. Meet with your below-grade-level students and your English language learners who need additional help to guide them as they work. If appropriate, have the small group select projects to work on together. Facilitate their learning by dividing up parts of the projects so that all students are engaged and working.

6 Give students time to complete their three activities. Provide students with materials like poetry books, art supplies, and old newspapers, magazines, or catalogs to help them complete their projects. Then, ask each student to choose one project to share with the class at an informal poetry reading.

7 If students finish early, they may complete the Anchor Activity.

Activity Levels
▲
Above Grade Level
■
On Grade Level
●
Below Grade Level

Assessment

Have students submit an exit slip answering the question *What was something new you learned about on the topic of poetry through your contract activities?* Review student responses to determine if the lesson objectives were met.

Anchor Activity

Have students research poetry to find a type of poem that is completely new to them. Have them collect at least two examples of this type of poetry. Then, have students write a poem of this type.

Name _____

Poetry Skills Vocabulary

Directions: Your teacher will assign you a word from the list below. Find an example and a definition to share with the class. Record your classmates' information on this chart, too.

Word	Definition	Example
alliteration		
assonance		
figurative language		
free verse		
homophone		
imagery		
metaphor		
onomatopoeia		
personification		
rhyme		
rhythm		
simile		
stanza		
tone		
verse		

Name _____

Poetry Skills Learning Contract

Directions: Read each activity carefully. Choose any three activities to complete by _____. Another option is to design your own activity, write a description of the activity, and ask your teacher to approve it.

1. Take three photos at school or bring in three photos from home. Write a metaphor or simile that describes each picture.

2. Recall the important events that have happened in your classroom or at your school this year. Use alliteration to write six newspaper headlines about those events. Beneath each headline, write a sentence that clarifies the topic.

3. Think about your favorite season. Fill a page with as many words and phrases as you can think of to describe that season. Then, write a descriptive poem to express your feelings about that time of year.

4. Close your eyes and picture a sport you like to play or watch. Listen to the sounds of the sport in your imagination. Do you hear the *splash* of your hands breaking the surface of the swimming pool? Do you hear the *thud* of linebackers colliding on the football field? Write a sports poem using onomatopoeia.

5. A song is a poem set to music. Use rhythm and rhyme to write a silly song. Choose a topic that inspires you, such as your pet, summer vacation, your least favorite food, or an embarrassing moment.

Choice 1 _____

Choice 2 _____

Choice 3 _____

I, _____, will complete these projects to the best of my ability by this date: _____.

Student signature: _____

Teacher signature: _____

Name _____

Poetry Skills Learning Contract

Directions: Read each activity carefully. Choose any three activities to complete by _____. Another option is to design your own activity, write a description of the activity, and ask your teacher to approve it.

1. Think about your family. Write a simile or metaphor that describes one of your family members. Illustrate your writing.

2. Use the skill of alliteration to describe five students who sit near you in class. Illustrate your writing.

3. Create a comic strip with five boxes. Draw characters and write speech and thought bubbles for them. Use onomatopoeia words in each box.

4. Write a poem in response to one of the following questions:

   Where do lightning bugs go during the day?

   What does a spider say to a fly?

   What is fluffy, blue, and makes a silly noise?

5. A song is a poem set to music. Use rhythm and rhyme to write a silly song. Choose a topic that inspires you, such as your pet, summer vacation, your least favorite food, or an embarrassing moment.

Choice 1 _____

Choice 2 _____

Choice 3 _____

I, _____, will complete these projects to the best of my ability by this date: _____.

Student signature: _____

Teacher signature: _____

Name _____

Poetry Skills Learning Contract

Directions: Read each activity carefully. Choose any three to complete by _____. Another option is to design your own activity, write a description of the activity, and ask your teacher to approve it.

1. Go on a simile scavenger hunt in poetry books. Find two similes. Copy the similes onto drawing paper and illustrate their meanings. *Hint: A simile is a comparison between two unrelated objects that uses the words **like** or **as**. Simile examples: He ran around the track like a cheetah. The gym was as hot as an oven.*

2. Cut out words from newspapers, magazines, and catalogs to create a sentence using alliteration. Glue the words to drawing paper. Draw a picture to go along with your phrase. *Hint: Alliteration is using a series of words that start with the same letter. Alliteration example: Hyper Harriet hopped home happily.*

3. Choose a poem that you enjoy. Illustrate one of the images in the poem.

4. Create a lift-the-flap book using onomatopoeia . Include five examples of onomatopoeic words along with drawings of the meanings. Put the word on top of the flap and an illustration beneath the flap. *Hint: Onomatopoeic words imitate sounds. Onomatopoeia examples: splash, crash, bang, plop, whoosh.*

5. A song is a poem set to music. Use rhythm and rhyme to write a silly song. Choose a topic that inspires you, such as your pet, summer vacation, your least favorite food, or an embarrassing moment.

Choice 1 _____

Choice 2 _____

Choice 3 _____

I, _____, will complete these projects to the best of my ability by this date: _____.

Student signature: _____

Teacher signature: _____

Place Value

Differentiation Strategy

Tiered Assignments

Standards

- Students will understand the meaning of place value in numbers.

- TESOL: Students will use appropriate learning strategies to construct and apply academic knowledge.

Materials

- lesson resources (pages 60–63)

- place value chart

- number cubes

Procedures

1 Display a place value chart in the room. Review the concept of place value with the whole class. Draw four blank lines on the board that can be filled in to make a four-digit number. Ask volunteers to come to the board to fill in the digits with any numbers they choose. Read the final number aloud together.

2 Turn the review into a challenge by asking students to come to the board to change one digit to make the number bigger. Ask another student to come to the board to change one digit to make the number smaller. Then, ask students to make specific changes to the number, such as reducing it by 100 or increasing it by 10.

3 Next, allow students to choose partners for a place value game called *Big*. Distribute copies of the *Big Game Card* activity sheet (page 60) to students.

4 To play *Big*, partners will take turns rolling a number cube. Students will place the numbers they roll on the blanks on the game card to form numbers. Once a number is written, it cannot be moved to another blank. For the first few rounds, the winner is the partner with the biggest number after all the digits have been recorded. After the first round of play, invite students to share the strategies they used for making big numbers.

5 After students have played several rounds, change the rules so that the winner is the partner with the *smallest* number. Ask students to discuss their strategies for making small numbers. Have students play several more rounds of the game. Observe students as they play to assess their understanding of the concept and determine the appropriate level of activity to assign.

6 Distribute copies of the *Playing with Place Value* activity sheets (pages 61–63) to students based on their readiness levels.

★ **English Language Support**—Pair these students with an English-proficient partner at the same readiness level. Ask English-proficient students to slowly and clearly read each box aloud and answer their partners' questions.

Place Value

❼ At the center of each tiered assignment sheet, you will see the *SPECIAL NUMBER* box. To make their special numbers, students with the triangle and square sheets will each roll a number cube and fill in the digits from left to right. Each student will have his or her own unique number. Students with the circle sheets should take turns rolling a die. They will make one number for all the circle group students. This will make it easier for them to support one another and for the teacher to assist them as they complete the activity sheet.

❽ If students finish early, they may complete the Anchor Activity.

Activity Levels
▲
Above Grade Level
■
On Grade Level
●
Below Grade Level

Assessment

Use the *Big Game Card* activity sheet (page 60) as a pre-assessment. Circulate around the classroom as students play the game and ask them to read the numbers that they create aloud to you and identify the place value of certain digits. If students struggle to work with four-digit numbers, assign the circle activity sheet; if they find the five-digit numbers a challenge, assign the square activity sheet. Those students who work easily with all the numbers may complete the triangle activity. You may wish to use the same game on the following day as a post-assessment.

Anchor Activity

Have students create a comic book about a superhero who saves people from their place value problems. They should include at least three different situations in the book and show how the hero saves the day.

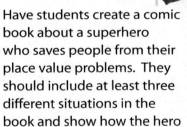

Name _____

Big Game Card

Directions: Play this game with a partner. Take turns rolling a number cube. Write the number you roll on any of the blanks. After you write the number, it cannot be moved. Take turns rolling and filling in the blanks until you have created a four-digit or five-digit number. Compare your number with your partner's number. Then, play again. You can play 10 times on this board.

1. _____ , _____ _____ _____

2. _____ , _____ _____ _____

3. _____ , _____ _____ _____

4. _____ , _____ _____ _____

5. _____ , _____ _____ _____

6. _____ , _____ _____ _____

7. _____ , _____ _____ _____

8. _____ , _____ _____ _____

9. _____ _____ , _____ _____ _____

10. _____ _____ , _____ _____ _____

Name _____

Playing with Place Value

Directions: Begin by creating your special number and writing it in the *SPECIAL NUMBER* box in the center of the board. Then, use the special number to complete each problem on a separate sheet of paper.

Write a riddle using place value clues to describe your special number.	How many numbers are less than your special number and greater than 43,427? What number is 25,000 more than your special number?	Create as many possible numbers as you can using the digits in your special number. Make a list in order from greatest to least.
Write out your special number in words. Give an example of where you might see this form of the number in real life.	**SPECIAL NUMBER:** __ __ , __ __ __	Add 50,000 to your special number. Write the new value of the ten thousands.
Write the special number in expanded form. Then, write another five-digit number below it in expanded form. Line up the digits. Add the numbers by first adding from top to bottom and then adding those totals from left to right.	Break your number apart in three ways using number sentences with more than two operations.	On the back of this paper, write a word problem using this number in a real-life situation.

Name _____

Playing with Place Value

Directions: Begin by writing the special number in the *SPECIAL NUMBER* box in the center of the board. Then, use the special number to complete each problem on a separate sheet of paper.

Use the digits in your special number to make the three smallest numbers possible.	Choose one number to place on either side of your special number. Write two statements using the < and > signs.	Use the digits in any order to make the three largest numbers possible.
Write out your special number in words.	**SPECIAL NUMBER:** __, __ __ __	Write the special number in expanded form.
Write the value of the largest digit and the smallest digit in your special number.	Break your number apart in three ways.	Write a sentence about your special number in a real-world example.

Name _____

Playing with Place Value

Directions: Begin by writing the special number in the *SPECIAL NUMBER* box in the center of the board. Then, use the special number to complete each problem.

Use the digits of your special number to make the smallest number possible. _____	Add any number to the thousands place (in front) of your special number. Is the new number greater than or less than your special number?	Use the digits to make the largest number possible. _____
Write out your special number in words. *Hint: Use a place value chart to help you.* _____ _____ _____	**SPECIAL NUMBER:** __ __ __	Write the special number in expanded form. _____ _____ _____
Write the value of each digit in your number. _____ _____ _____	Round the special number to the nearest thousand. _____	Draw a picture of someone using the special number in real life.

Rounding and Estimation

Differentiation Strategy

 Kaplan's Depth and Complexity

Standards

- Students will understand how to use specific strategies to estimate answers and check the reasonableness of results.

- TESOL: Students will use appropriate learning strategies to construct and apply academic knowledge.

Materials

- lesson resources (pages 66–69)

- index cards

- videos or picture books on rounding and estimation (*See page 167.*)

- tape

- art supplies

Procedures

Preparation Note: Make a large number line on the board from zero to 100, marking intervals of 10. On separate index cards, write a two-digit number between 10 and 100. Make at least one index card per student.

★ **English Language Support**—Show a video or read a picture book to these students that will help them make connections between rounding and estimation skills and real-life situations.

1 Begin class by placing an index card facedown on each student's desk. Call on one student to show his or her card to the class. Have the student choose a volunteer to round the number to the nearest 10. Then, have the volunteer tape the index card to the board below its rounded form on the number line. For example, 47 would round to 50, so the index card with 47 on it should be taped below number 50 on the number line.

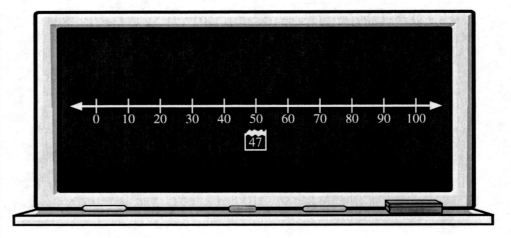

2 The volunteer will then show his or her card to the class and choose the next volunteer to place it on the board. Play continues until all numbers have been taped to the board.

3 After the rounding review, tell students that they will continue to practice their rounding and estimating skills. By answering important questions about the topic, they will gain a deeper understanding of the skill.

Rounding and Estimation

❹ Distribute copies of the *Questions About Rounding and Estimating* activity sheets (pages 66–68) to students based on their readiness levels. Explain to students that they will be answering questions and completing related tasks. Allow students to work independently or to choose a partner who has the same activity sheet.

❺ Decide ahead of time how many questions and tasks you want students to answer and complete. Ask students to choose their question or questions. Have students complete their work on a separate sheet of paper. Provide students with art supplies to help them complete their tasks.

❻ If students finish early, they may complete the Anchor Activity.

Activity Levels
▲
Above Grade Level
■
On Grade Level
●
Below Grade Level

Assessment

After students finish their assignment, distribute copies of the *Reflection Letter* activity sheet (page 69). Allow students time to reflect on their learning and complete this self-assessment.

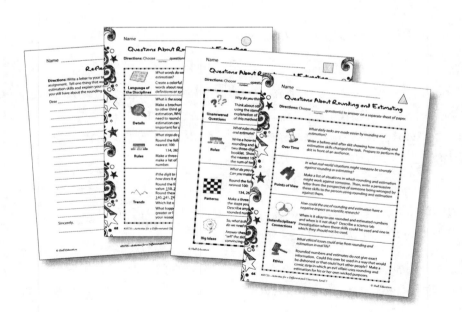

Anchor Activity

Have students create a rounding and estimation game using situations from the real lives of third graders. Challenge them to think about the ways they might use estimation at school, in sports, with friends, or at home. They should make a game board and game pieces.

Name _____

Questions About Rounding and Estimating

Directions: Choose _____ question(s) to answer on a separate sheet of paper.
(number)

Over Time

What daily tasks are made easier by rounding and estimation?

Write a before-and-after skit showing how rounding and estimation skills changed the task. Prepare to perform the skit in front of an audience.

Points of View

In what real-world situations might someone be strongly against rounding or estimating?

Make a list of situations in which rounding and estimation might work against someone. Then, write a persuasive letter from the perspective of someone being wronged by these skills to the person using rounding and estimation against them.

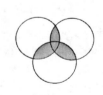

Interdisciplinary Connections

How could the use of rounding and estimation have a negative impact on scientific research?

When is it okay to use rounded and estimated numbers and when is it not okay? Describe a science lab investigation where these skills could be used and one in which they should not be used.

Ethics

What ethical issues could arise from rounding and estimation in real life?

Rounded numbers and estimates do not give exact information. Could this ever be used in a way that would be dishonest or that could hurt other people? Make a comic strip in which an evil villain uses rounding and estimation for his or her own wicked purposes.

Name _____

Questions About Rounding and Estimating

Directions: Choose _____ question(s) to answer on a separate sheet of paper.
_(number)

Unanswered Questions

Why do you think someone created a method for rounding?

Think about other ways to arrive at an estimate without using the standard *Rounding Rule*. Write a clear explanation of another method. Show several examples of this method in action.

Rules

What rules must someone understand to be able to round and estimate?

Write a how-to booklet that clearly explains the rules for rounding and estimation to other third graders. Choose two three-digit numbers to use as examples in your booklet. Show the reader how to round these numbers to the nearest 10 and the nearest 100, and how to estimate the sum of two numbers.

Patterns

What do you notice about rounded and estimated numbers? Can you make any generalizations?

Round the following numbers to the nearest 10 and the nearest 100:

134, 263, 178, 345, 452, 658, 109, 253, 899, 921

Make a three-column chart to organize your work. List the steps you repeat every time you round a number. Describe any patterns you see when you compare the rounded numbers to the original numbers.

Big Ideas

So, what is the big deal with rounding and estimation? Why do we need to know how to use these skills?

Answer these questions in an advertising flyer designed to "sell" the skills of rounding and estimation. Be creative in convincing customers to "buy" into the ideas.

Name _____

Questions About Rounding and Estimating

Directions: Choose _____ question(s) to answer on a separate sheet of paper.
(number)

**Language of the Disciplines**	*What words do we need to understand about rounding and estimation?* Create a colorful abstract poster that includes important words about rounding and estimation and simple definitions or symbols for the words.
Details	*What is the scoop on rounding and estimation?* Make a brochure that explains rounding and estimation to other third graders. Include WHO uses rounding and estimation, WHAT rounding and estimation are, WHEN you need to round or estimate numbers, WHERE rounding and estimation can be found in the real world, and WHY it is important for us to understand it.
Rules	*What steps do you take to round a number?* Round the following numbers to the nearest 10 and the nearest 100: 134, 263, 178, 345, 452, 658, 109, 253, 899, 921 Make a three-column chart to organize your work. Then, make a list of the steps you repeat every time you round a number.
Trends	*If the digit to the right of the number being rounded is a five, how does it affect the accuracy of the estimate?* Round the following numbers to the underlined place value: 150, 251, 75, 15, and 1,500. Round these numbers to the underlined place value: 140, 241, 74, 14, and 1,400. Which list of estimates is more accurate? What happens if this is a list of 100 numbers? Is the effect greater or less than a smaller group of numbers? Explain your reasoning and show examples that prove your claim.

Name _____

Reflection Letter

Directions: Write a letter to your teacher. Tell one thing you liked about the assignment. Tell one thing that was challenging. Rate your own rounding and estimation skills and explain your rating. End the letter by asking a question you still have about the rounding and estimation.

Dear _____,

_____

_____

_____

_____

_____

_____

_____

_____

_____

_____

_____

_____

_____

Sincerely,

_____

Multiplication Strategies

Differentiation Strategy

Leveled Learning Contracts

Standards

- Students will understand the effect of multiplication on the size and order of numbers.

- TESOL: Students will use English to obtain, process, construct, and provide subject matter information in spoken and written form to achieve academically in all content areas.

Materials

- lesson resources (pages 72–75)
- index cards
- color tiles
- graph paper
- playing cards
- number cubes
- hundreds chart
- base-ten blocks
- counters
- multiplication flash cards
- magazines
- grocery store flyers

Procedures

Note: This particular lesson uses leveled learning contracts to differentiate the content and process of instruction. It is intended to help implement differentiation while using other instructional resources (for example, a core mathematics program). This lesson will span several days.

1 Assess students' knowledge of multiplication strategies by conducting a pre-test. Be sure the assessment covers the use of sets, arrays, and base-ten blocks to solve simple multiplication problems.

2 Evaluate students' pre-tests and prepare a *Multiplication Strategies Outline* activity sheet (page 72) for each student. Students who need extra support will attend the whole-class lessons and activities, as well as complete the contract activities as homework assignments. Instead of participating in a whole-class lesson or guided practice, students who have already mastered a concept will work independently on the activities listed on their learning contracts. Attach the appropriate leveled *Multiplication Strategies Learning Contract* (pages 73–75) to each student's outline.

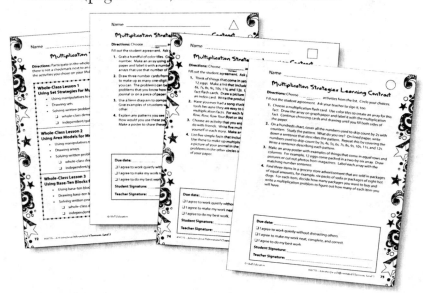

3 Draw a web or circle map on the board. Ask students to brainstorm what they know about multiplication. Highlight the following vocabulary terms related to multiplication: *factor*, *product*, and *array*.

Multiplication Strategies

4 Explain to students that they will be learning about multiplication for the next several days. Distribute to each student their *Multiplication Strategies Outline* and contract packet. All students should receive a contract packet so that they can see which topic(s) they contracted out of (even if it is none). This is also a great way to give students an outline of your unit of study.

5 Review the *Multiplication Strategies Outline* and the leveled contracts with students and clarify the time line for participating in whole-group lessons and completing the independent contract tasks. Set a due date for the contract projects. Provide students with the necessary manipulatives to help them complete their tasks.

★ **English Language Support**—Read aloud the project choices to these students. Help them choose projects appropriate for their abilities. If necessary, partner them with English-proficient students as they complete the activities.

6 Begin your unit of study. Lessons should flow in this order:

- Using Set Strategies for Multiplication
- Using Area Models for Multiplication
- Using Base-Ten Blocks for Multiplication

7 If students finish early, they may complete the Anchor Activity.

Assessment

Use the following guidelines to evaluate student work on their learning contracts:

- Followed project guidelines
- Demonstrated an understanding of multiplication
- Calculated accurately
- Completed assignment on time

Activity Levels
▲
Above Grade Level
■
On Grade Level
●
Below Grade Level

Anchor Activity

Have students read the book *The Best of Times* by Greg Tang. Challenge them to make their own "Best of Times" books. Ask them to include any hints or strategies that help them remember each set of facts. On the back cover, have them add a checklist to track the facts as they master them.

Name _____

Multiplication Strategies Outline

Directions: Participate in the whole-class activities that are checked below. If there is not a checkmark next to an activity, you can use that time to work on the activities you chose on your *Multiplication Strategies Learning Contract*.

Whole-Class Lesson 1
Using Set Strategies for Multiplication

- Using manipulatives to create groups
- Drawing sets
- Solving written problems
  - ❏ whole-class demonstration lesson and discussion
  - ❏ independent/guided practice

Whole-Class Lesson 2
Using Area Models for Multiplication

- Using manipulatives to create arrays
- Drawing arrays
- Solving written problems
  - ❏ whole-class demonstration lesson and discussion
  - ❏ independent/guided practice

Whole-Class Lesson 3
Using Base-Ten Blocks for Multiplication

- Using base-ten blocks to model multiplication
- Drawing base-ten blocks
- Solving written problems
  - ❏ whole-class demonstration lesson and discussion
  - ❏ independent/guided practice

Name _____

Multiplication Strategies Learning Contract

Directions: Choose _____ activities from the list. Circle your choices.
(number)
Fill out the student agreement. Ask your teacher to sign it, too.

1. Grab a handful of color tiles. Count the tiles and write down the total number. Make an array using all of the tiles. Draw the array on graph paper and label it with a number sentence. Repeat this for all possible arrays that use that number of tiles.

2. Draw three number cards from a deck of playing cards. Use the numbers to make up as many one-digit and two-digit multiplication problems as you can. The problems can be one-step or two-step problems. Solve the problems that you know how to work. Record the others in your math journal or on a piece of paper for further investigation.

3. Use a Venn diagram to compare and contrast addition and multiplication. Give examples of situations where you would choose to use one or the other.

4. Explain any patterns you see in the sets of multiplication facts from 0 to 12. How would you use these patterns to help you solve other problems? Make a poster to share these patterns and strategies with other students.

Due date: _____

❑ I agree to work quietly without distracting others.

❑ I agree to make my work neat, complete, and correct.

❑ I agree to do my best work.

Student Signature: _____

Teacher Signature: _____

Name _____

Multiplication Strategies Learning Contract

Directions: Choose _____ activities from the list. Circle your choices.
(number)
Fill out the student agreement. Ask your teacher to sign it, too.

1. Think of things that come in sets. For example, two shoes, five fingers, and 12 eggs. Make a list that includes something that comes in 2s, 3s, 4s, 5s, 6s, 7s, 8s, 9s, 10s, 11s, and 12s. Use these examples to create multiplication fact flash cards. Draw a picture of the set and write the fact on one side of an index card. Write the product (answer) on the other side.

2. Have you ever had a song stuck in your head? Songs make great memory tools because they are easy to learn! Choose four hard-to-remember multiplication facts. For each fact, write a song to a familiar tune, such as *Row, Row, Row Your Boat* or *Mary Had a Little Lamb*.

3. Choose an activity that you enjoy. Think of sports, hobbies, and things you do with friends. Write five multiplication stories about the activity. Include yourself in each story. Make an answer key for the problems.

4. List five simple facts that include a number about your favorite animal. Use these to make up multiplication problems about your animal. Draw a picture of your animal in the center of an idea web. Write the math problems in the other circles on the web. Make an answer key on the back of your paper.

Due date: _____

❏ I agree to work quietly without distracting others.

❏ I agree to make my work neat, complete, and correct.

❏ I agree to do my best work.

Student Signature: _____

Teacher Signature: _____

Name _____

Multiplication Strategies Learning Contract

Directions: Choose _____ activities from the list. Circle your choices.
(number)
Fill out the student agreement. Ask your teacher to sign it, too.

1. Choose a multiplication flash card. Use color tiles to create an array for this fact. Draw the array on graph paper and label it with the multiplication fact. Continue choosing cards and drawing until you fill both sides of the paper.

2. On a hundreds chart, cover all the numbers used to skip count by 2s with counters. Study the pattern. What do you see? On lined paper, write down a sentence that describes the pattern. Repeat this by covering the numbers used to skip-count by 3s, 4s, 5s, 6s, 7s, 8s, 9s, 10s, 11s, and 12s. Write a sentence describing each pattern.

3. Make an array poster with examples of things that come in equal rows and columns. For example, 12 eggs come packed in a two-by-six array. Draw pictures or cut out photos from magazines. Label each array with the matching number sentence.

4. Find three items in a grocery store advertisement that are sold in packages of equal amounts, for example, six-packs of soda or packages of eight hot dogs. For each item, decide how many packages you want to buy and write a multiplication problem to figure out how many of each item you will have.

Due date: _____

❏ I agree to work quietly without distracting others.

❏ I agree to make my work neat, complete, and correct.

❏ I agree to do my best work.

Student Signature: _____

Teacher Signature: _____

Playing with Fractions

Differentiation Strategy

 Menu of Options

Standards

- Students will understand the concept of fractions and be able to identify and name fractional parts.
- TESOL: Students will use appropriate learning strategies to construct and apply academic knowledge.

Materials

- lesson resources (pages 78–81)
- fraction cards
- digital camera
- sentence strips
- index cards
- playing cards
- graph paper
- glue
- art supplies
- plastic storage bags
- video camera
- magazines
- number cube template (cube.pdf)

Procedures

❶ This lesson is designed for students who have already been introduced to the three models of fractions—parts of a whole, parts of a set, and placed on a number line. It is intended to broaden and deepen students' understanding of fraction concepts.

★ **English Language Support**—Provide English language learners with fraction cards that show pictures of fractions as parts of a whole, parts of a set, and placed on a number line.

❷ Tell students that math plays a big part in most sports. Ask students to brainstorm connections between fractions and football (equal parts of the field, quarters of the game, halftime, player statistics, and equal parts of the team). Have them think-pair-share their ideas with classmates seated nearby. Then, ask volunteers to share ideas with the whole class.

❸ Explain to students that they will get to choose their own "plays" in order to help them score a "touchdown" while practicing their fraction skills. Distribute copies of the *Fraction Playbook Menu of Options* activity sheets (pages 78–80) to students. Read the activity choices aloud to students. Point out that in a football game, certain plays are better matches for certain players. The same is true in learning, because certain activities are a better fit for some students than others.

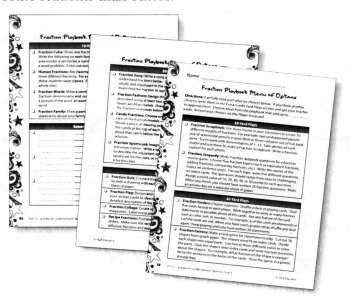

Playing with Fractions

4 Have students think-pair-share their ideas for the activities that are the best fit for them. Give below-grade-level students and English language learners the option of working in pairs.

5 Distribute copies of the *Player Scorecard* activity sheet (page 81) to students. Explain that it will be used to help students make a game plan. Use sample plays to model how to complete the chart. Determine the number of "yards" (points) students will need to attempt. Set a due date for the projects.

6 Remind students to choose plays that add up to the number of points required. Circulate and assist students in making good choices from the menu of options and completing the *Player Scorecard* correctly. Provide students with the materials needed to help them complete their activities.

7 Give students time to complete the activities. When they are finished, allow time for them to present their game-winning projects to the class. After each project is presented, give the student "three cheers" by asking three students to share a positive comment about the project.

8 If students finish early, they may complete the Anchor Activity.

Assessment

Evaluate each of the students' projects and record the points they earn on the *Player Scorecard* activity sheet under "Yards Gained." You may want to create a rubric to help students understand the components you will be evaluating, such as completeness, creativity, and neatness. Provide specific feedback for students in the "Teacher Comments" section of the *Player Scorecard* activity sheet.

Anchor Activity

Have students brainstorm all the possible fractions that can be used to describe themselves, for example, *I am $\frac{1}{4}$ of my family*. They can then use the fractions to write and illustrate a *My Life in Fractions* autobiography.

Name _____

Fraction Playbook Menu of Options

Directions: Carefully read each play (or choice) below. If you think of other choices, write them in the Extra-Credit Yard Plays section and get your teacher to approve them. Choose plays from the playbook that add up to _____ yards. Record your choices on the *Player Scorecard*.

50-Yard Plays

❏ **Fraction Scrapbook:** Use items found in your classroom to create 10 different models of fractions. For example, two unsharpened pencils out of seven total pencils in your desk or three red pens out of five total pens. Try to work with denominators of 1–12. Take photos of each model and use them to make a Fraction Scrapbook. Write a fraction caption for each photo.

❏ **Fraction Jeopardy:** Write *Fraction Jeopardy* questions for a fraction review game. Choose five fraction topics (such as equivalent fractions, adding fractions, comparing fractions, etc.). Write the names of the topics on sentence strips. For each topic, write five different questions on index cards. The questions should range from easy to challenging. Assign a point value of 10, 20, 30, 40, or 50 points to each question. When you finish, you should have written 25 fraction questions. Make an answer key on a separate sheet of paper.

40-Yard Plays

❏ **Fraction Finders:** Choose a partner. Shuffle a deck of playing cards. Deal five cards faceup to each player. Work together to write as many fraction statements as possible about all the cards. Use any feature of the card, such as color, suit, or number. For example, $\frac{3}{10}$ *of the cards are diamonds* or $\frac{2}{5}$ *of the cards are red*. When you have used up your ideas, shuffle and deal again. Keep playing until you have written 20 statements.

❏ **Fraction Factory:** Make a card game for classmates to play. Cut out 10 shapes from graph paper. The shapes must fit on index cards. Divide each shape into equal parts. Use two or three different colors to color the parts. Glue the shapes onto index cards and write fraction questions about the shapes. For example, *What fraction of the shape is orange?* Write the answers on the backs of the cards. Store the game in a plastic storage bag.

Fraction Playbook Menu of Options *(cont.)*

30-Yard Plays

☐ **Fraction Song:** Write a song about a specific fraction to help others understand fractions better. Use the words *numerator, denominator, whole,* and *equal part* in the song. Include examples of where you might find the fraction in real life.

☐ **Fraction Fashion:** Design three pieces of jewelry that could each be described using at least two different fractions. For example, $\frac{2}{3}$ *of the beads are blue crystals.* Draw and color a picture of each piece. Write the fraction sentences below each item.

☐ **Candy Fractions:** Choose one type of candy to use as an example for each of the fraction models—parts of a whole, parts of a set, and length. Divide a piece of drawing paper into three sections. Draw a picture of the candy at the top of each section. Write a fraction word problem about that candy below the picture. Then, draw a picture to show the solution.

☐ **Fraction Sportscast:** Imagine that you are a sports announcer for a television station. Write a sportscast that uses at least five fractions to describe the important sporting events of the day. Perform your sportscast for the class, or videotape yourself reading the news and play it for the class.

20-Yard Plays

☐ **Fraction Quiz:** Create a true/false quiz with at least 15 statements. Include a drawing with each question. Make an answer key on another sheet of paper.

☐ **Fraction Flag:** Design and color a flag for a new country. Make sure your design could be described using fractions. Use fractions to write a detailed description of the flag.

☐ **Fraction Collage:** Create a collage of fractions using pictures cut from magazines. Label every picture with the fraction it shows.

☐ **Recipe Fractions:** Find and copy the recipe for one of your favorite dishes. Make sure the recipe has more than one fraction. Compare the different fractions and explain the differences in amounts.

Fraction Playbook Menu of Options (cont.)

10-Yard Plays

❑ **Fraction Cube:** Show one fraction in many ways by making a 3-D cube. Write the following on each face of the cube—the fraction, a shaded area model, a set model, a number line model, a real-world example, and a word problem. Color, cut out, and assemble your cube.

❑ **Human Fractions:** Ask classmates to help you make models of at least three different fractions. For example, $\frac{2}{5}$ *of these students are girls* or $\frac{1}{3}$ *of these students wear glasses.* Show your human fraction examples to the whole class.

❑ **Fraction Words:** Make a word web for the words *equal part, whole, fraction, denominator,* and *numerator.* Include a meaning of the word, a picture of the word, an example of the word, and a nonexample of the word.

❑ **Fraction Family:** Draw a portrait of your family. Write three true statements about your family, using fractions.

Extra-Credit Yard Plays

❑ _____
_____
_____
_____

❑ _____
_____
_____
_____

❑ _____
_____
_____
_____

Name _____

Player Scorecard

Directions: Complete the chart below to make your game plan. Under *Player's Choices*, list the activities that you plan to complete. Under *Yards Attempted*, list the points that each activity is worth. Make sure that all the activities add up to _____ yards. Your teacher will fill in the *Yards Gained* column with the points that you earn. The assignments must be completed by _____.

Player's Choices	Yards Attempted	Yards Gained	Equipment Needed
Total Yards:			
Teacher Comments:			

Finding Perimeter

Differentiation Strategy

 Discovery Learning

Standards

- Students will understand the basic measures of perimeter, area, volume, capacity, mass, angle, and circumference.

- TESOL: Students will use English to interact in the classroom.

Materials

- lesson resources (pages 84–87)

- *Spaghetti and Meatballs for All* by Marilyn Burns

- chart paper and markers

- one-inch color tiles

- beans or centimeter cubes

- one-inch graph paper

Procedures

1 Begin the lesson by reading aloud the picture book *Spaghetti and Meatballs for All* by Marilyn Burns. It is a mathematical story about a family trying to seat 32 dinner guests at a table.

2 Place students in homogeneous groups of three to four students. Tell students that they will work cooperatively to solve a similar problem. The problem they will solve is one that could happen in a real-world business setting. They will use discovery learning, or inquiry methods, to solve the problem.

3 Display the *Open for Business* activity sheet (page 84). Read it aloud to the class. Ask students to turn to someone sitting nearby and rephrase the problem in their own words. Clarify the problem as needed.

4 Distribute copies of the *Take Your Pick* activity sheet (page 85) to students. Assign groups a shape based on their readiness levels. Have groups choose a restaurant that matches their assigned shape.

5 Distribute sheets of chart paper to groups. Give students time to invent a restaurant name and draw a picture of their business at the top of the paper.

6 Next, bring the class back together as a whole group. Distribute copies of the *Seating Chart Challenge* activity sheet (page 86) to students. Read the challenge together and discuss the materials available. Show students how to represent a square table with a color tile. Show how a bean can be used to represent a person sitting on one side of the table. Model an example of an ice cream shop that has three square tables. Show one example of how tables could be arranged with two pushed together and one separate.

7 Review the Rules for Table Groups on the *Seating Chart Challenge* activity sheet (page 86). Model how you would draw your arrangement on graph paper to create a seating chart. Discuss and record how many total customers could be seated at each table and how many could be seated in all.

Finding Perimeter

8 Write the word *perimeter* on the board. Explain that perimeter is the distance around the outside of a shape. Ask students to picture a fence around a backyard.

★ **English Language Support**—Work with these students to make vocabulary graphic organizers for the term *perimeter*. Have them fill out a two-by-two chart for the word with sections for the definition, an illustration, a real-world example, and a nonexample.

9 Distribute one-inch color tiles, beans or centimeter cubes, and one-inch graph paper to groups. Allow time for students to complete the project to make their posters.

10 If students finish early, they may complete the Anchor Activity.

Assessment

During the next class period, have students review their work and respond to the questions on the *Restaurant Reflections* (page 87) so that you can assess what they learned.

Activity Levels
▲
Above Grade Level
■
On Grade Level
●
Below Grade Level

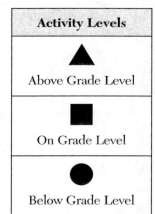

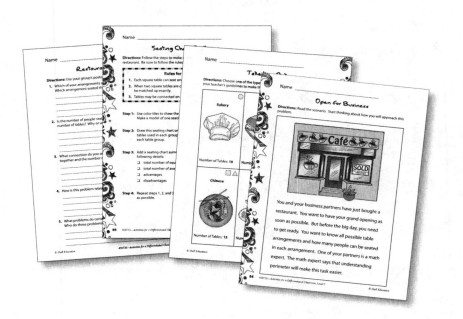

Anchor Activity

Have students write perimeter word problems about real-world situations. These could be used as math review game questions at the end of the lesson or unit.

Name _____

Open for Business

Directions: Read the scenario. Start thinking about how you will approach this problem.

You and your business partners have just bought a

restaurant. You want to have your grand opening as

soon as possible. But before the big day, you need

to get ready. You want to know all possible table

arrangements and how many people can be seated

in each arrangement. One of your partners is a math

expert. The math expert says that understanding

perimeter will make this task easier.

Name _____

Take Your Pick

Directions: Choose one of the types of restaurants for your project. Follow your teacher's guidelines to make the best choice for your group.

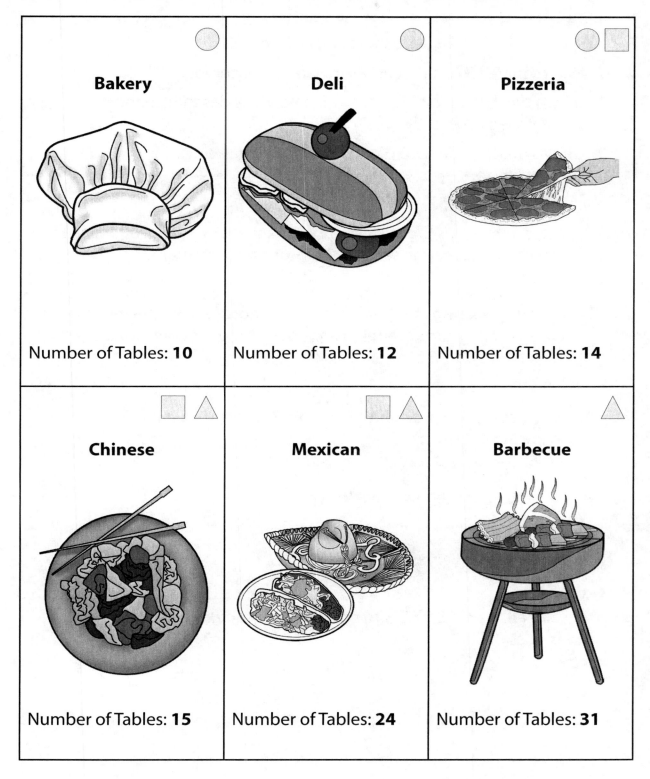

Bakery

Number of Tables: **10**

Deli

Number of Tables: **12**

Pizzeria

Number of Tables: **14**

Chinese

Number of Tables: **15**

Mexican

Number of Tables: **24**

Barbecue

Number of Tables: **31**

Name _____

Seating Chart Challenge

Directions: Follow the steps to make all possible seating arrangements for your restaurant. Be sure to follow the rules for table groups.

┌───┐
│   **Rules for Table Groups**   │
│   │
│   1. Each square table can seat one person on each side. │
│   │
│   2. When two square tables are connected, the sides that connect must │
│   be matched up exactly.   │
│   │
│   3. Tables may be connected on one, two, or three sides. │
└───┘

Step 1: Use color tiles to show the number of square tables in your restaurant. Make a model of one seating chart for your restaurant.

Step 2: Draw this seating chart on your group's poster. Label the number of tables used in each grouping and the number of seats available at each table group.

Step 3: Add a seating chart summary to the poster. Include the following details:

  ❑ total number of square tables

  ❑ total number of available seats

  ❑ advantages

  ❑ disadvantages

Step 4: Repeat steps 1, 2, and 3 to make as many different seating charts as possible.

Name _____

Restaurant Reflections

Directions: Use your group's poster project to answer the questions.

1. Which of your arrangements seated the smallest number of people? Which arrangement seated the most people?

   _____
   _____
   _____
   _____

2. Is the number of people seated always the same when using the same number of tables? Why or why not?

   _____
   _____
   _____
   _____

3. What connection do you see between the number of tables joined together and the number of people seated at that table group?

   _____
   _____
   _____
   _____

4. How is this problem related to perimeter?

   _____
   _____
   _____
   _____

5. What problems do certain seating arrangements create for your business? Who do these problems affect? What could you do to fix these problems?

   _____
   _____
   _____

Symmetry

Differentiation Strategy

 Leveled Learning Centers

Standards

- Students will understand that symmetry is a basic property of a figure and be able to recognize and identify lines of symmetry.

- TESOL: Students will use appropriate learning strategies to construct and apply academic knowledge.

Materials

- lesson resources (pages 90–93)

- Materials for centers (*See Preparation Note.*)

- markers

- rulers

- audio recorder

Procedures

Preparation Note: Cut out two paper shapes for each student. One shape should show symmetry and the other shape should not. Use a die-cut machine or cut simple shapes from a pattern.

Set up three learning centers in the classroom. Each center should have enough space for six to ten students to work. Copy the *Symmetry Centers* activity sheets (pages 90–92) and post them at the appropriate station. Each card contains leveled activities. Place the following supplies at each center:

- **Center 1 (Letter Symmetry)**—blank paper; paper bags filled with letter tiles such as *Scrabble®* tiles; small mirrors with straight edges; symmetrical, die-cut letters, such as *A*, *B*, *C*, *D*, *E*, and *H*; index cards; rulers

- **Center 2 (Shape Symmetry)**—colored construction paper cut into fourths; pattern blocks; timers; geoboards; rubber bands; dot paper; blank paper; scissors; glue; poster board

- **Center 3 (Real-World Symmetry)**—paper plates; white construction paper; magazines; art supplies; poster board; scissors; glue

① Give each student two shapes, one symmetrical and one asymmetrical. Have students fold the asymmetrical shape in half. Ask if the two halves cover each other exactly. Explain that because they do not, the shape is not symmetrical. Have students label that shape *no symmetry*. Next, have students fold the symmetrical shape in half. Explain that because the two halves cover each other exactly, the shape is symmetrical. Have students label that shape *symmetry*.

② On the symmetrical shape, have students trace the line of symmetry with a dark marker. Instruct them to label this with the words *line of symmetry*.

③ Explain to students that they will explore three learning centers that focus on symmetry. Assign students a shape based on their readiness levels. Explain that students should choose center activities that match that particular shape.

4 Give students time to explore the three centers. Allow students to choose their own starting points in the rotation. The only limitation is that they must choose a station with an available seat or workspace. Ask students to carefully read the directions. Teach them the "ask three, then me" rule. When following this rule, students must ask three classmates for help before asking the teacher for help. This encourages independence during center activities.

★ **English Language Support**—Use audio software to record yourself reading the center instructions slowly. Allow the English language learners to listen to your directions as they work.

5 If students finish early, they may complete the Anchor Activity.

Assessment

Use the *Symmetry Centers Rubric* (page 93) to assess students' work.

Activity Levels
★
English Language Learner
▲
Above Grade Level
■
On Grade Level
●
Below Grade Level

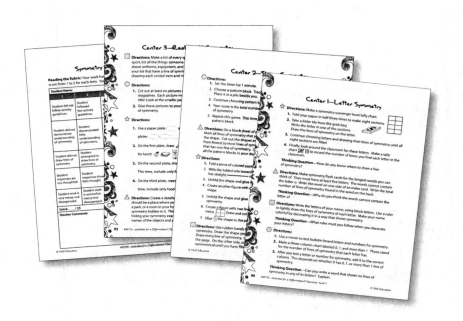

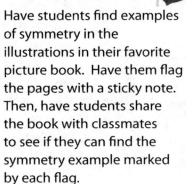

Anchor Activity

Have students find examples of symmetry in the illustrations in their favorite picture book. Have them flag the pages with a sticky note. Then, have students share the book with classmates to see if they can find the symmetry example marked by each flag.

Center 1—Letter Symmetry

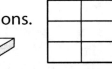 

☆ **Directions:** Make a symmetry scavenger hunt tally chart.

1. Fold your paper in half three times to make eight sections.

2. Take a letter tile from the grab bag. Write the letter in one of the sections. Draw the lines of symmetry on the letter.

3. Continue choosing letters and drawing their lines of symmetry until all eight sections are filled.

4. Finally, look around the classroom for these letters. Make a tally chart ||||| ||| to record the number of times you find each letter in the classroom.

Thinking Question—How do you know where to draw a line of symmetry?

△ **Directions:** Make symmetry flash cards for the longest words you can think of. They must have at least five letters. The words cannot contain the letter *o*. Write the word on one side of an index card. Write the total number of lines of symmetry found in the word on the back.

Thinking Question—Why do you think the words cannot contain the letter *o*?

▢ **Directions:** Write the letters of your name, using block letters. Use a ruler to lightly draw the lines of symmetry of each letter. Make your name colorful by decorating it in a way that shows symmetry.

Thinking Question—What rules must you follow when you decorate your letters?

◯ **Directions:**

1. Use a mirror to test bulletin board letters and numbers for symmetry.

2. Make a three-column chart labeled *0, 1,* and *more than 1.* These stand for the number of lines of symmetry that each letter has.

3. After you test a letter or number for symmetry, add it to the correct column. This depends on whether it has 0, 1, or more than 1 line of symmetry.

Thinking Question—Can you write a word that shows no lines of symmetry in any of its letters? Explain.

Center 2—Shape Symmetry

Directions:

1. Set the timer for 1 minute.

2. Choose a pattern block. Trace it on paper. Draw one line of symmetry. Place it in a pile beside you.

3. Continue choosing pattern blocks to trace and draw until time runs out.

4. Your score is the total number of blocks you traced and marked with a line of symmetry.

5. Repeat this game. This time, draw all the lines of symmetry for each pattern block.

Directions: On a blank sheet of paper, trace around each type of pattern block. Mark all lines of symmetry that you find for each shape. Write the number inside the shape. Cut out the shapes and glue them to construction paper in order from fewest to most lines of symmetry. Use the pattern blocks to make a design that has one line of symmetry. Count the total number of lines of symmetry in all the pattern blocks in your design.

Directions:

1. Fold a piece of colored paper in half.

2. With the folded side toward you as the base of your shape, draw a figure that has straight —————— sides. Cut ✂ out your shape.

3. Unfold the shape and glue it to a poster. Draw and label its line of symmetry.

4. Create another figure with only curved ⌒ sides. Cut ✂ out your shape.

5. Unfold the shape and glue 🖊 it to a poster. Draw and label its line of symmetry.

6. Create a figure with two lines of symmetry by folding a piece of paper in half twice. Draw and cut ✂ out the shape.

7. Glue 🖊 the shape to the poster. Draw and label the lines of symmetry.

Directions: Use rubber bands to make a shape on the geoboard that shows symmetry. Draw the shape you made on one side of a piece of dot paper. Draw every line of symmetry. Continue creating examples until you have filled the page. On the other side, create and draw examples of shapes that are not symmetrical until you have filled the page.

Center 3—Real-World Symmetry

☐ **Directions:** Make a list of every sport that comes to mind. Next to each sport, list all the things someone needs or uses to play the sport. Think about uniforms, equipment, and the playing field. Circle all the items on your list that have a line of symmetry. Create a sports symmetry poster by drawing each circled item and marking its line of symmetry.

◯ **Directions:**

1. Cut out at least six pictures of people, animals, and objects from magazines. Each picture must have at least one line of symmetry. *Hint: Look at the smaller parts of pictures as well as the whole picture.*

2. Glue these pictures to your paper. Draw and label the lines of symmetry.

☆ **Directions:**

1. Use a paper plate ◯ as a pattern to trace three

   plates ◯◯◯ on your poster.

2. On the first plate, draw ✏ and label a picture of every item you ate

   for lunch 🍎🥪🥛. Draw any lines of symmetry that you see.

3. On the second plate, draw and label a healthy meal 🍎🥪🥛.

   This time, include only foods that have lines of symmetry. ◯

4. On the third plate, create another healthy meal 🍎🥪🥛. This

   time, include only foods that *do not* have lines of symmetry. ◯

△ **Directions:** Create a detailed, colorful seek-and-find scene. The scene should be a place where you enjoy spending time, such as a favorite store, a park, or a room in your house. It must have at least 10 examples of symmetry hidden in it. Think carefully about your illustration. Be creative in hiding your symmetry examples. Make an answer key on the back. List the names of the objects and sketch the outlines to show the lines of symmetry.

Symmetry Centers Rubric

Reading the Rubric: Your work has been graded on five criteria. You earned a score from 1 to 5 for each item. Your work is worth a total of 25 points.

Student Name:				
1	**2**	**3**	**4**	**5**
Student did not follow activity guidelines.	Student followed few activity guidelines.	Student followed some activity guidelines.	Student followed most activity guidelines.	Student followed activity guidelines completely.
Student did not demonstrate understanding of symmetry.	Student demonstrated little understanding of symmetry.	Student demonstrated some understanding of symmetry.	Student demonstrated significant understanding of symmetry.	Student demonstrated extensive understanding of symmetry.
Student did not draw lines of symmetry.	Student attempted to draw lines of symmetry.	Student drew some lines of symmetry correctly.	Student drew most lines of symmetry correctly.	Student drew all lines of symmetry correctly.
Student responses are not thoughtful.	Student responses show little thought.	Student responses are somewhat thoughtful.	Student responses are thoughtful and mostly complete.	Student responses are thoughtful and complete.
Student work is very messy and disorganized.	Student work is somewhat messy and disorganized.	Student work is fairly neat and careful.	Student work is mostly neat and careful.	Student work is very neat and careful.

Score: _____ / 25

Teacher Comments:

States of Matter

Leveled Learning Centers

Standards

- Students will understand that matter has different states, all matter has distinct properties, and some materials can change from one state to another through heating and cooling.

- TESOL: Students will use appropriate learning strategies to construct and apply academic knowledge.

Materials

- lesson resources (pages 96–99)

- materials for centers (*See Preparation Note.*)

- mini vocabulary word wall

- science notebooks

- labels

Procedures

Preparation Note: Prepare for the lesson ahead of time by setting up three learning centers in the classroom. Each center should have enough space for six to ten students to work. Copy the *States of Matter Centers* activity sheets (pages 96–98) and post them at each station. Place the following materials at the centers:

- **States of Matter Center 1 (Make a Mixture)**—large bowls filled with three different cereals; three scoops; two pan balances with gram measures for mass; Internet

- **States of Matter Center 2 (Melting Matter)**—ice cubes; small plastic dishes or clear containers (two per pair); thermometers; timers; pencils; paper; masking tape; markers (freeze ice cubes in trays that will give them uniform size and shape)

- **States of Matter Center 3 (Property Sort)**—bead necklaces; small paper bags filled with 10 objects with a variety of physical properties, such as game pieces, math manipulatives, paper clips, rubber bands, marbles, coins, tennis balls, yarn, and pipe cleaners

★ **English Language Support**—Make a mini vocabulary word wall of important words and pictures to serve as a reference for these students. Make copies, laminate them, and post them at each center.

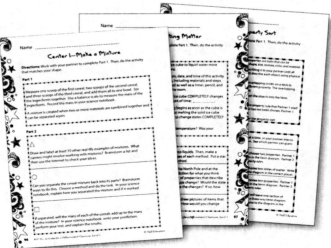

States of Matter

1 Have students record their notes in a science notebook. Begin the lesson by asking students to list as many examples of matter as they can think of in 30 seconds. After 30 seconds pass, tell students to stop writing and share their list with a partner. Allow a few students to share their lists with the entire class.

2 Tell students that they will be participating in centers about the states of matter. Distribute labels marked with triangles, squares, and circles to students based on their readiness levels. Instruct students to place their labels on the inside cover in their science notebooks. Explain that they will complete activities that match the shapes on their labels. Then, pair students of similar readiness levels for the center activities.

3 Instruct students to record their center data and results in their science notebooks. Have them title a section in their notebooks, "States of Matter Centers."

4 Give students time to explore the three centers. Allow pairs to choose their own starting points in the rotation. The only limitation is that they must choose a station with an available seat or workspace. Ask students to carefully read the center directions. Teach them the "ask three, then me" rule. When following this rule, students must ask three classmates for help before asking the teacher for help. This encourages independence during center activities.

5 If students finish early, they may complete the Anchor Activity.

6 At the end of the lesson, bring the class back together and ask students to share what they learned at each station.

Assessment

Ask questions of students while they are working to assess their understanding of the concepts. Use the *States of Matter Centers Checklist* (page 99) to document your observations.

Activity Levels
Above Grade Level
On Grade Level
Below Grade Level

Anchor Activity

Have students write a story about a day in the life of an ice cube. Ask students to name the ice cube and give it a distinct personality. Have them write about how the ice cube feels as he or she experiences each state of matter.

Name _____

Center 1—Make a Mixture

Directions: Work with your partner to complete Part 1. Then, do the activity that matches your shape.

Part 1

Measure one scoop of the first cereal, two scoops of the second cereal, and three scoops of the third cereal, and add them all to one bowl. Stir the ingredients together. Use a balance scale to measure the mass of the ingredients. Record the mass in your science notebook.

A *mixture* is created when two or more materials are combined together and can be separated again.

Part 2

△ Draw and label at least 10 other real-life examples of mixtures. What careers might involve working with mixtures? Brainstorm a list and then use the Internet to check your ideas.

○ Can you separate the cereal mixture back into its parts? Brainstorm ways to do this. Choose a method and do the task. In your science notebook, explain how you separated the mixture and if it worked.

☐ If separated, will the mass of each of the cereals add up to the mass of the mixture? In your science notebook, write your prediction, perform your test, and explain the results.

Name _____

Center 2—Melting Matter

Directions: Work with your partner to complete Part 1. Then, do the activity that matches your shape.

Part 1

Your Mission: Change the state of a solid ice cube to liquid water more quickly than it changes at room temperature.

In your science notebook, record the location, date, and time of this activity. Write your plan for completing this mission, including materials and steps to follow. Gather the materials that you need as well as a timer, pencil, and paper. Record the current temperature of the room.

At a room temperature of _____ , an ice cube COMPLETELY changes from a solid to a liquid in the following amount of time: _____.

Take an ice cube from frozen storage. Timing begins as soon as the cube is removed. Carry out your planned method for melting the solid ice cube and record the exact amount of time it takes to change states COMPLETELY from a solid to a liquid.

Was your method faster or slower than room temperature? Was your prediction correct? Why or why not?

Part 2

☐ List all the ways you could change solids into liquids. Then, make a chart to show the advantages and disadvantages of each method. Put a star beside the one you think would be the best method.

△ Imagine that you placed a cup of water at the North Pole and at the equator. In your science notebook, write a prediction for what you think would happen to each cup of water. Make a list of properties that describe each cup. Would the amount of matter in the cups change? Would the state of matter in the cups change? Could you reverse the changes? If so, how would you do it?

○ Use a cause-and-effect graphic organizer to draw pictures of items that change from solid to liquid when heat is added. How would you change these substances from a liquid back into a solid?

Name _____

Center 3—Property Sort

Directions: Work with your partner to complete Part 1. Then, do the activity that matches your shape.

Part 1

Matter has different **physical properties**. Physical properties are traits that can be experienced through the five senses. These include shape, size, texture, color, and material.

Take turns choosing an object from the bag and describing it to your partner until all items in the bag have been described. Then, you will describe each object using physical property traits.

Next, do a property sort. Lay the bead necklaces in overlapping circles on a desk to create a Venn diagram. Each circle will stand for a different property. The overlapping section will contain objects that have both properties.

Partner 1—Choose two properties and use them to sort the objects into the Venn Diagram.

Partner 2—Look at the objects and try to figure out the property rule that Partner 1 used for each section. After three tries, if the correct answer has not been chosen, Partner 1 should reveal the rule used.

Repeat the activity, with Partner 2 choosing the rule for the property sort.

Part 2

○ Start with an empty Venn diagram. Add one item at a time, as your partner tries to guess the rules each time an object is added to a section. See which partner can guess the other's rules the fastest.

☐ Partner 1 should examine the items in the bag and choose two properties. Partner 1 will pull items from the bag one at a time and place them in the Venn diagram. Partner 2 will look at the objects and try to guess the physical property rules.

In your science notebook, draw a Venn diagram. Then, choose two states of matter. Write a state of matter in each circle. Add at least 10 items to the diagram in the correct places.

△ Partner 1 should examine the items in the bag and choose two properties. Partner 1 will pull items from the bag one at a time and place them in the Venn diagram. Partner 2 will look at the objects and try to guess the physical property rules.

Try the game again. This time, choose two properties that will leave one section of the Venn diagram empty. In your science notebook, draw a three-way Venn diagram. Write a property in each of the sections. Add at least 10 items to the diagram in the correct places.

States of Matter Centers Checklist

Teacher Directions: Use the checklist below to assess students' performance. Use checkmarks (✔) in the criteria columns to indicate proficiency.

Student Name	Follows directions	Stays on task	Shows understanding of mixtures	Shows understanding of states of matter	Shows understanding of physical properties

Forces of Motion

Differentiation Strategy

 Discovery Learning

Standards

- Students will understand the relationship between the strength of a force and its effect on an object.
- TESOL: Students will use English to interact in the classroom.

Materials

- lesson resources (pages 102–105)
- photos of beaches
- scissors
- glue
- science notebooks
- audio or video podcast software
- index cards
- sand and containers
- small toy vehicles
- model-making materials

Procedures

❶ Begin the lesson by showing students postcards or photos of beach scenes. Ask students if they have ever played on a beach. Invite them to share stories of unexpected events or problems that happened at the beach.

❷ Explain to students that they will be working on a solution to a problem that happened at a beach. The activity will require them to work in cooperative groups to solve the problem.

❸ Place students in small heterogeneous groups of three or four. Distribute copies of the *Stuck in the Sand* activity sheet (page 102) to students. Have students cut out and glue the scenario into their science notebooks and sketch a picture of the problem.

❹ Distribute copies of the *Forces of Motion Group Challenge* activity sheet (page 103) to students. Read the directions aloud to the whole class. Clarify the expectations and answer students' questions.

★ **English Language Support**—Give these students an audio or video podcast of the *Stuck in the Sand* scenario (page 102) and the *Forces of Motion Group Challenge* activity sheet (page 103).

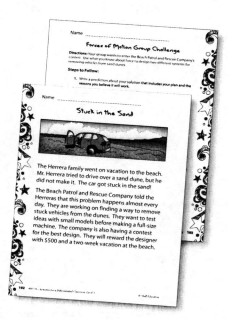

Forces of Motion

⑤ Distribute copies of the *Rules to Remember* and *Key Words* activity sheet (page 104) to students. Review this with students, and instruct them to cut out and glue these items into their science notebooks.

⑥ Read the rules aloud to the class. After each rule, have students think-pair-share with a partner about what it means and how they will apply it.

⑦ Ask students to discuss the vocabulary words with their groups. Have each group use index cards to make one set of vocabulary cards. The cards should include the word, its meaning in their own words, and an illustration of the word.

⑧ Give each group a container filled with sand. Students will use this to model the sand dune scenario and try several possible solutions. Students will work together to complete the *Forces of Motion Group Challenge* activity sheet (page 103).

⑨ Invite each group to present one solution to the class.

⑩ If students finish early, they may complete the Anchor Activity.

Assessment

Use the *Forces of Motion Rubric* (page 105) to assess students' projects.

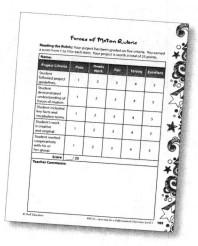

Anchor Activity

Have students design experiments to test the effectiveness of each solution under different conditions. Suggest that they try different sizes of vehicles, different materials, and wet and dry sand.

Name _____

Stuck in the Sand

The Herrera family went on vacation to the beach. Mr. Herrera tried to drive over a sand dune, but he did not make it. The car got stuck in the sand!

The Beach Patrol and Rescue Company told the Herreras that this problem happens almost every day. They are working on finding a way to remove stuck vehicles from the dunes. They want to test ideas with small models before making a full-size machine. The company is also having a contest for the best design. They will reward the designer with $500 and a two-week vacation at the beach.

Name _____

Forces of Motion Group Challenge

Directions: Your group wants to enter the Beach Patrol and Rescue Company's contest. Use what you know about force to design two different systems for removing vehicles from sand dunes.

Steps to Follow:

1. Write a prediction about your solution that includes your plan and the reasons you believe it will work.

2. Draw a diagram of your solution. Label the parts.

3. List materials needed to test the solution.

4. Locate and gather your materials.

5. Create a model and test your solution.

6. Record your results.

Group Questions:

1. Is the force you used a push, a pull, or both? Mark the type of force used on your diagram.

2. What are the advantages and disadvantages of each solution? Create a T-chart to list them.

3. How could the materials you used be made large enough for a full-size model?

4. Compare the results of your two solutions. Based on this information, which one should you propose?

5. How would combining ideas from each of your systems affect the results?

6. In what other real-life situations could your system be used?

Name _____

Rules to Remember

A force is a push or a pull.

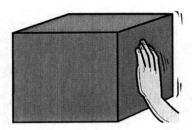

A force changes
the position of an object.

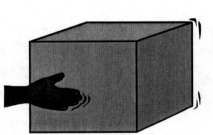

Motion is caused by a force.

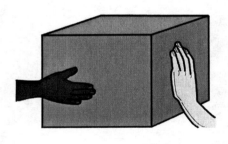

Magnetism and
gravity are forces.

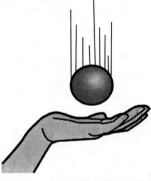

Key Words

cause	position
effect	push
force	pull
gravity	strength
magnet	work
motion	

© *Shell Education*

Forces of Motion Rubric

Reading the Rubric: Your project has been graded on five criteria. You earned a score from 1 to 5 for each item. Your project is worth a total of 25 points.

Name:					
Project Criteria	**Poor**	**Needs Work**	**Fair**	**Strong**	**Excellent**
Student followed project guidelines.	1	2	3	4	5
Student demonstrated understanding of forces of motion.	1	2	3	4	5
Student included key facts and vocabulary terms.	1	2	3	4	5
Student's work is creative and original.	1	2	3	4	5
Student worked cooperatively with his or her group.	1	2	3	4	5
Score	____/ 25				

Teacher Comments:

Earth's Shifting Surface

Differentiation Strategy

Leveled Learning Contracts

Standards

- Students will understand how the features on Earth's surface are constantly changed by a combination of forces and processes.

- TESOL: Students will use English to obtain, process, construct, and provide subject matter information in spoken and written form.

Materials

- lesson resources (pages 108–111)

- video clips or photos, books and websites about earthquakes, volcanoes, and landslides *(See page 167.)*

- music

- online visual glossaries

- chart paper

- card stock

- index cards

Procedures

❶ Begin the lesson by showing video clips or photos of earthquakes, volcanoes, and landslides.

❷ After showing the video clips, have students "mill to music." Ask students to move around the room while a song plays. Stop the music suddenly. When this happens, students must pair with a classmate nearby to share ideas about how earthquakes change Earth's surface. Repeat the "mill to music" activity for volcanoes and landslides.

❸ Tell students that they will have an opportunity to choose activities from a list of projects about Earth's shifting surface.

❹ Distribute copies of the *Earth's Shifting Surface Learning Contracts* activity sheets (pages 108–110) according to student readiness levels. Then, have students choose three projects to complete. Set a deadline for when these projects are due. Also, decide if these projects will be completed at home or during class.

Earth's Shifting Surface

5 Make reference materials, such as textbooks, magazines, library books, and computers with bookmarked websites, available to students as they work. Have students keep track of the resources that they use on their learning contracts.

★ **English Language Support**—Have several computers available to display visual glossaries of important vocabulary terms.

6 Give students time to complete three activities. Provide students with any needed materials to help them complete the activities. Then, ask each student to choose one project to share with the class during small-group time.

7 If students finish early, they may complete the Anchor Activity.

Assessment

Use the *Earth's Shifting Surface Rubric* (page 111) to assess students' projects. Be sure to show this to students before they begin working on their projects so that they understand the criteria that you will be evaluating.

Activity Levels
▲
Above Grade Level
■
On Grade Level
●
Below Grade Level

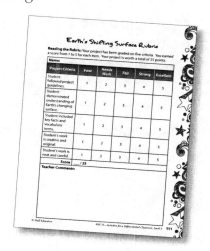

Anchor Activity

Have students write a job description for a seismographer and describe the use of seismograph equipment to measure earthquakes.

Name _____

Earth's Shifting Surface Learning Contract

Directions: Choose three of the following activities to complete. Place a checkmark (✔) next to your choices. Sign the contract and ask your teacher to sign it, too.

❑ If you had to choose between living in a place affected by landslides, earthquakes, or volcanoes, which would you choose? Explain your choice. Make a checklist of things that you would have to do to be prepared and stay safe.

❑ Research the construction of earthquake-safe buildings. Sketch a design for your own earthquake-safe house. Label the special features and describe how they protect it.

❑ Make a set of rules that are true for each of the following changes to Earth's surface: volcanic eruption, earthquake, and landslide.

❑ Make a crossword puzzle using 10 key words from your study of Earth's changing surface.

❑ Create a postcard with a detailed picture of a landform on the front. Close your eyes and imagine your view from the center of this landform. On the back, write a note to a friend describing the landform in vivid details.

❑ Research recent earthquake activity to find the eight most recent earthquakes. Make a chart that includes the location, the time, the date, and the strength of each one. List them on the chart from the strongest to weakest. Make a list of any patterns or trends you notice.

I, _____, will complete these projects to the best of my ability by this date: _____.

List the resources you used to complete your activities:

_____

_____

_____

Student Signature: _____

Teacher Signature: _____

Name _____

Earth's Shifting Surface Learning Contract

Directions: Choose three of the following activities to complete. Place a checkmark (✔) next to your choices. Sign the contract and ask your teacher to sign it, too.

❑ Imagine that you are a newspaper reporter at the scene of a major landslide, earthquake, or volcano. Write a short news article for your local newspaper. Reporters try to answer *who, what, why, when, where,* and *how* questions about news events. They put the most important information first.

❑ Draw a cutaway diagram of an erupting volcano. Label its parts. Write a caption that explains what causes the volcano to erupt.

❑ Read a nonfiction book about one of the forces that causes a sudden change to the surface of Earth. Make a glossary of terms from the book. Include the most important words you need to know about your topic. Write kid-friendly definitions and put the words in alphabetical order.

❑ Draw a Venn diagram to compare two forces that change the surface of Earth.

❑ Create a concentration-type game that includes sets of three matching cards with the name of the rapid change or landform, a picture of the rapid change or landform, and your own definition of the rapid change or landform.

❑ Find one example of each of the following landforms on a map. Make a chart to show the name and location of each: *mountains, hills, valleys,* and *plains.*

I, _____, will complete these projects to the best of my ability by this date: _____.

List the resources you used to complete your activities:

_____

_____

_____

Student Signature: _____

Teacher Signature: _____

Name _____

Earth's Shifting Surface Learning Contract

Directions: Choose three of the following activities to complete. Place a checkmark (✔) next to your choices. Sign the contract and ask your teacher to sign it, too.

❑ Draw before-and-after pictures on separate index cards that show a location before and after an event that changed the surface of Earth. Write the event that caused the change on a third card. Make a set of each type of card. Invite classmates to match the correct before-and-after cards.

❑ Imagine that you are a photographer who has traveled the world photographing different landforms. Make two scrapbook pages that show photos of four different landforms. Your scrapbook pages should include photos, titles, captions, journaling, and other details.

❑ Make a cause-and-effect graphic organizer to explain the effects of a volcano, earthquake, or landslide on Earth's surface. Include words and pictures.

❑ Draw a comic strip that shows a cartoon character going through an earthquake, volcano, or landslide. Include information from before, during, and after the event.

❑ Create a picture dictionary for younger students using simple drawings and explanations of 10 important words related to earthquakes, volcanoes, and landslides.

I, _____, will complete these projects to the best of my ability by this date: _____.

List the resources you used to complete your activities:

_____

_____

_____

Student Signature: _____

Teacher Signature: _____

Earth's Shifting Surface Rubric

Reading the Rubric: Your project has been graded on five criteria. You earned a score from 1 to 5 for each item. Your project is worth a total of 25 points.

Name:					
Project Criteria	**Poor**	**Needs Work**	**Fair**	**Strong**	**Excellent**
Student followed project guidelines.	1	2	3	4	5
Student demonstrated understanding of Earth's changing surface.	1	2	3	4	5
Student included key facts and vocabulary terms.	1	2	3	4	5
Student's work is creative and original.	1	2	3	4	5
Student's work is neat and careful.	1	2	3	4	5
Score	___ / 25				
Teacher Comments:					

Blast Off to Space

Differentiation Strategy

 Menu of Options

Standards

- Students will understand that Earth is one of several planets that orbit the sun, and the moon orbits Earth.

- TESOL: Students will use English to obtain, process, construct, and provide subject matter information in spoken and written form.

Materials

- lesson resources (pages 114–117)
- bulletin-board paper
- sticky notes
- audio recorder
- science notebooks
- art supplies
- slide show software
- books and websites about the solar system (See page 167.)
- index cards
- card stock

Procedures

Preparation Note: Make a large chart on bulletin-board paper. Title it *Solar System*. Divide the chart into five columns. Label them *We Think…*, *We Know…*, *Oops!*, *We Learned…*, and *We Wonder…*.

1 Distribute several sticky notes to each student. Tell them that a *claim* is something that we think we know. We cannot prove it until we collect more evidence. Have students write their claims about the solar system on sticky notes. Tell them that they do not need to write their names on the sticky notes. This anonymity can help alleviate fear of incorrect claims.

2 Collect the sticky notes and place them under the *We Think . . .* column. Eliminate duplicates. Encourage students to make more claims if you notice that a subject has not been covered.

3 Once all claims have been added to the chart, read them aloud to the class. Then, explain to students that they will be using a menu of options to complete activities about the solar system. Explain that as they are working on their activities, they can add new information to the chart. If evidence is found to prove that one of the claims is true or false, they should attach the evidence to the claim and place it in the new column where it belongs.

4 Distribute copies of the *Blast Off to Space Menu of Options* activity sheets (pages 114–115) to students. Read the directions and the menu aloud to the whole class. Decide ahead of time how many rocket-fuel credits (points) students must complete from the menu. Explain that when they complete the predetermined number of points, they will be able to send their rocket into space.

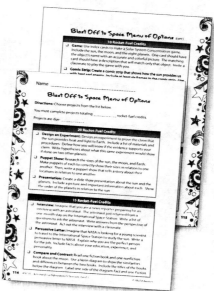

Blast Off to Space

5 Distribute copies of the *Blast Off to Space: Mission Planning Chart* activity sheet (page 116) to students. Circulate around the room and assist students as they make their choices and fill out their charts. Make sure that the English language learners and the below-grade-level students understand the activities and choose appropriately.

★ **English Language Support**—Provide these students with an audio recording device to replace written responses with verbal responses.

6 Give students time to complete their projects. Provide students with any needed materials to help them complete their activities. Encourage students to continue adding to the *Solar System* chart. If they discover that a claim is actually untrue, they can move the claim to the *Oops!* column. Each day, discuss changes to and new information on the chart. Encourage students to discuss possible reasons why people believe those statements in the *Oops!* column. This is a good opportunity to point out how science is constantly changing.

7 When all projects are finished, review the chart one final time. Move the remaining *We Think . . .* statements without evidence to the *We Wonder . . .* column. Students should add any other questions that they still have to this column. Have students record the chart's information in their science notebooks.

8 If students finish early, they may complete the Anchor Activity.

Assessment

Make one copy of the *Blast off to Space Rubric* (page 117) for each student. Use the three rubrics to evaluate students' work on each of their projects separately. Total each student's points for all projects for a final grade.

Anchor Activity

Have students find out why Pluto is not considered a planet anymore. Then, have them take a stance on this topic. Students should write a letter to the class as if Pluto could talk, explaining their stance.

Name _____

Blast Off to Space Menu of Options

Directions: Choose projects from the list below.

You must complete projects totaling _____ rocket-fuel credits.

Projects are due: _____

20 Rocket-Fuel Credits

❑ **Design an Experiment:** Design an experiment to prove the claim that the sun provides heat and light to Earth. Include a list of materials and procedures. Define how you will know if the evidence supports your claim. Write hypotheses about what this same experiment would show if done on two other planets.

❑ **Puppet Show:** Research the sizes of the sun, the moon, and Earth. Make puppets of each to correctly show their sizes in relation to one another. Then, write a puppet show that tells a story about their locations in relation to one another.

❑ **Presentation:** Create a slide show presentation about the sun and the planets. Include a picture and important information about each. Show the order of the planets in relation to the sun.

15 Rocket-Fuel Credits

❑ **Interview:** Imagine that you are a news reporter preparing for an interview with an astronaut. The astronaut just returned from a one-month stay on the International Space Station. Write a list of questions to ask the astronaut. Write answers from the perspective of the astronaut. Act out the interview with a classmate.

❑ **Persuasive Letter:** Imagine that NASA is looking for a young scientist to travel to the International Space Station to study the sun. Write a persuasive letter to NASA. Explain why you are the perfect person for the job. Include facts about your education, experience, and personality.

❑ **Compare and Contrast:** Read one fiction book and one nonfiction book about the moon. Use a Venn diagram to show the similarities and differences between the two books. Include the titles of the books below the diagram. Label one side of the diagram *Fact* and one *Fiction*.

Blast Off to Space Menu of Options (cont.)

10 Rocket-Fuel Credits

❑ **Game:** Use index cards to make a Solar System Concentration game. Include the sun, the moon, and the eight planets. One card should have the object's name with an accurate and colorful picture. The matching card should have a description that will match only that object. Invite a classmate to play the game with you.

❑ **Comic Strip:** Create a comic strip that shows how the sun provides us with heat and energy. Include at least six frames in the comic strip. Use dialogue or thought bubbles in each box.

❑ **Postcards:** Imagine how life would change if the sun burned out. Create two postcards. One should have a picture of your town and a note about your life *before* the sun burned out. The other postcard should have a picture of your town and a note about life *after* the sun burned out.

❑ **Trading Cards:** Create a set of planet trading cards. On each card, include a detailed picture of the planet, information about its size and distance from the sun, and at least two important facts.

❑ **Riddle:** Write riddles for eight important objects in the solar system. Fold an index card in half. Write the riddle on the outside and the answer on the inside.

5 Rocket-Fuel Credits

❑ **Summary:** Find information in at least two nonfiction books about what the sun provides to Earth. Write a summary of the information you found. Check for correct spelling, punctuation, and grammar.

❑ **Poem:** Write a poem about the sun. Include its characteristics, location, and what it provides to Earth. Consider writing an acrostic, a haiku, a diamante, a cinquain, or any other type of poem. Write your poem on white paper. Decorate it with a border or illustration.

❑ **Model:** Make signs that say *Sun*, *Moon*, and *Earth*. Ask three classmates to hold them. Organize them into a human model of their orbits.

❑ **Song:** Using a familiar tune, such as *Row, Row, Row Your Boat*, write a song that will help others remember the order of the planets.

Name _____

Blast Off to Space Mission Planning Chart

Directions: To blast off to space, you need to earn at least _____
(number)
rocket-fuel credits. (Choose activities from the menu of options that add up to that number of points.) Record your choices in the chart. Any extra fuel credits earned will serve as bonus fuel for your voyage.

Project Name	Points	Materials Needed
Project 1		
Project 2		
Project 3		

Total Points: _____

Name _____

Blast Off to Space Rubric

Directions: Use the rubrics below to assess the three projects.

Project 1: _____

The project indicates an understanding of the topic.	no	some	yes
The project contains accurate facts.	no	some	yes
The project fulfills the assignment requirements.	no	some	yes
The project represents the student's full potential.	no	some	yes
Comments:			

Project 2: _____

The project indicates an understanding of the topic.	no	some	yes
The project contains accurate facts.	no	some	yes
The project fulfills the assignment requirements.	no	some	yes
The project represents the student's full potential.	no	some	yes
Comments:			

Project 3: _____

The project indicates an understanding of the topic.	no	some	yes
The project contains accurate facts.	no	some	yes
The project fulfills the assignment requirements.	no	some	yes
The project represents the student's full potential.	no	some	yes
Comments:			

Total Score: _____

Science

Creature Features

Differentiation Strategy

 Tiered Assignments

Standards

- Students will understand that many characteristics of animals are inherited from its parents, and other characteristics are learned.
- TESOL: Students will use appropriate learning strategies to construct and apply academic knowledge.

Materials

- lesson resources (pages 120–123)
- photos of recognizable people (celebrities, professional athletes, or teachers from the school)
- scissors
- drawing materials
- glue
- science notebooks

Procedures

1 Begin the lesson by displaying several photos of recognizable people, such as celebrities, professional athletes, or teachers from the school. Describe one of the people by mentioning only inherited traits. These include eye color, hair color, hair texture, skin tone, number of fingers, and number of eyes. Ask students to guess the person you described.

2 Have students choose a partner for the next activity. Tell partners to sit across from each other. Give students 30 seconds to write the name of their partner and a physical description of him or her. Remind students to use only inherited traits and not clothing or accessories in their descriptions.

3 Have students crumple up their descriptions and toss them anywhere in the room. Ask students to pick up one paper and choose a new partner. The partners will take turns reading the descriptions and guessing the subjects. They should then give the paper to the person whom they think it describes. If some students get more than one paper, the whole class must help match the descriptions to the correct student.

4 Explain to students that we use traits to describe people and objects. Physical traits describe appearance. Write the words *trait, inherited, behavior, learned, and function* on the board. Explain the meaning of each word and provide examples. (See the answer key for page 120 on the Teacher Resource CD for suggested definitions.)

5 Distribute copies of the *Creature Features Vocabulary Chart* activity sheet (page 120) to students. Have students complete the vocabulary chart for the five words on the board.

© *Shell Education*

Creature Features

6 Distribute copies of the *Inherited or Learned?* activity sheets (pages 121–123) to students based on their readiness levels.

7 Ask students with the triangle and square activity sheets to read the directions carefully. Read the directions aloud to students with the circle sheets. Then, model for the whole class how to complete the graphic organizer.

★ **English Language Support**—Meet with these students to review the meanings and pictures of the vocabulary words. Have students act out the meaning of the words for each other.

8 Students will complete the graphic organizers. Then they will cut along the dotted lines to create flip charts. Next, students should draw a picture on the front of each flap to represent the words underneath the flap.

9 Give students time to share one favorite item from their flip charts in a gallery walk. Then, have students glue the assignment into their science notebooks or display them on a bulletin board.

10 If students finish early, they may complete the Anchor Activity.

Assessment

Evaluate students' work to determine whether or not the lesson objective was met. Prepare mini-lessons to reteach the concepts to small groups as necessary.

Activity Levels
▲
Above Grade Level
■
On Grade Level
●
Below Grade Level

Anchor Activity ⚓

Have students read the book *I Wish I Had Duck Feet* by Dr. Seuss. Ask them to choose an animal trait that they wish they had. Have them write a story about how the trait helps them to survive in a specific environment.

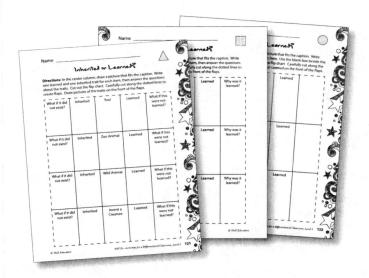

Name _____

Creature Features Vocabulary Chart

Directions: Complete the chart using the vocabulary words from the lesson.

Vocabulary Word	My Definition	Picture
trait		
inherited		
behavior		
learned		
function		

Name _____

Inherited or Learned?

Directions: In the center column, draw a picture that fits the caption. Write one learned and one inherited trait for each item, then answer the questions about the traits. Cut out the flip chart. Carefully cut along the dotted lines to create flaps. Draw pictures of the traits on the front of the flaps.

What if it did not exist?	Inherited	You!	Learned	What if this were not learned?
What if it did not exist?	Inherited	Zoo Animal	Learned	What if this were not learned?
What if it did not exist?	Inherited	Wild Animal	Learned	What if this were not learned?
What if it did not exist?	Inherited	Invent a Creature	Learned	What if this were not learned?

Name _____

Inherited or Learned?

Directions: In the center column, draw a picture that fits the caption. Write one learned and one inherited trait for each item, then answer the questions about the traits. Cut out the flip chart. Carefully cut along the dotted lines to create flaps. Draw pictures of the traits on the front of the flaps.

How is it useful?	Inherited	You!	Learned	Why was it learned?
How is it useful?	Inherited	Zoo Animal	Learned	Why was it learned?
How is it useful?	Inherited	Wild Animal	Learned	Why was it learned?

#50735—*Activities for a Differentiated Classroom, Level 3* © *Shell Education*

Name _____

Inherited or Learned?

Directions: In the center column, draw a picture that fits the caption. Write one learned and one inherited trait for each item. Use the blank box beside the list to draw pictures of the traits. Cut out the flip chart. Carefully cut along the dotted lines to create flaps. Write *Inherited* or *Learned* on the front of the flaps.

Picture	Inherited	You!	Learned	Picture
Picture	Inherited	Pet	Learned	Picture
Picture	Inherited	Zoo Animal	Learned	Picture

Science

Who Swallowed Whom?

Differentiation Strategy

 Kaplan's Depth and Complexity

Standards

- Students will understand how changes in the environment have different effects on organisms.

- TESOL: Students will use appropriate learning strategies to construct and apply academic knowledge.

Materials

- lesson resources (pages 126–129)

- *There Was an Old Lady Who Swallowed a Fly* by Simms Taback

- chart paper and markers

- science notebooks

- scissors

- glue

- tape

- one-inch strips of construction paper in a variety of colors

- books, websites, pictures and diagrams about food chains and ecosystems *(See page 167.)*

Procedures

★ **English Language Support**—Preteach English language learners by having them read an informational picture book at their reading level about food chains. Explain important words and show students pictures and diagrams of food chains. Have them copy a food-chain diagram into their science notebooks.

❶ Begin the lesson by reading, watching, or listening to *There Was an Old Lady Who Swallowed a Fly* by Simms Taback. Discuss the humor in the song and whether it could really happen. Ask students if there is anything in the song that could happen in real life.

❷ Introduce and explain the term *food chain*. Make a true/false T-chart on chart paper so students can organize the ideas from the song by scientific accuracy.

❸ Place students in five heterogeneous groups. Assign each group one of the following ecosystems: desert, ocean, forest, arctic, and pond. Give each group a one-inch-wide strip of construction paper in a different color.

❹ Distribute copies of the *Animal Clip Art* activity sheet (page 126) to students. Students will create food chains using the clip art on this sheet. Have students cut out the clip art and glue the animal images to the construction paper strips in order from the top of the food chain to the bottom.

❺ Have each group display its completed food chain on a bulletin board. The chains should branch out from a large sun in the center of the board.

Who Swallowed Whom?

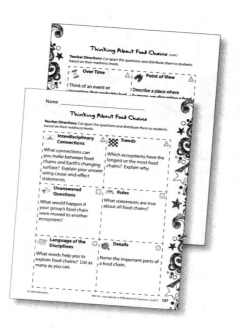

6. Explain to students that they will answer thoughtful questions about food chains. Cut apart the questions on the *Thinking About Food Chains* activity sheets (pages 127–128) and distribute them to students according to their readiness levels. Have students write their answers in complete sentences on separate 4 x 4–inch squares of construction paper or card stock. Group members who finish early can work together to create a labeled drawing of their food chain on another blank square.

Activity Levels	
▲	Above Grade Level
■	On Grade Level
●	Below Grade Level

7. Each group will tape its completed squares together to form two cubes (there are six faces on each of the two cubes). When every group has assembled its cubes, groups should trade cubes and take turns rolling and reading the responses of other groups.

8. If students finish early, they may complete the Anchor Activity.

Assessment

Distribute copies of the *Food Chain Comic Strip Assessment and Rubric* (page 129) to students in order to assess and evaluate what they learned in this lesson. Students must show in a creative format their understanding of the food chain and how animals, plants, and the sun interact to make the food chain work.

Anchor Activity

Have students research another food chain that is new to them. Ask them to write and illustrate a picture book modeled after *There Was an Old Lady Who Swallowed a Fly*. Their artwork and wording can be humorous, but the basic story should be based on facts.

Name _____

Animal Clip Art

Directions: Cut apart the pictures below. Use them to create your food chain.

mesquite pod	horned lizard	harvester ant	hawk	sun
whale	plankton	herring	seal	sun
rabbit	bear	grass	fox	sun
clam	squid	plankton	penguin	sun
water beetle	pond plant	duck	tadpole	sun

Name _____

Thinking About Food Chains

Teacher Directions: Cut apart the questions and distribute them to students based on their readiness levels.

 Interdisciplinary Connections

What connections can you make between food chains and Earth's changing surface? Explain your answer using cause-and-effect statements.

 Trends

Which ecosystems have the longest or the most food chains? Explain why.

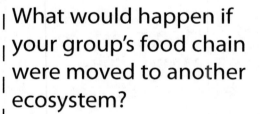 **Unanswered Questions**

What would happen if your group's food chain were moved to another ecosystem?

 **Rules**

What statements are true about all food chains?

 Language of the Disciplines

What words help you to explain food chains? List as many as you can.

 Details

Name the important parts of a food chain.

Thinking About Food Chains *(cont.)*

Teacher Directions: Cut apart the questions and distribute them to students based on their readiness levels.

 Over Time △

Think of an event or invention that probably had an impact on food chains. Explain your idea.

 Point of View △

Describe a place where humans are disrupting a food chain. If people know they are disrupting the food chain, why do you think they would continue? How might they explain their point of view?

 Ethics ☐

Is it ever okay for humans to make changes to the environment that will destroy part of a food chain? Explain why or why not.

 Over Time ☐

What would happen if one species in a food chain became extinct? Explain your prediction.

 Patterns ○

How can you tell the order of animals and plants in a food chain? How can you predict what comes next?

 Big Ideas ○

Why is it important to learn about food chains?

Name _____

Food Chain Comic Strip Assessment

Directions: Choose any ecosystem from this lesson. Use what you have learned to create an original comic strip about any of the food chains studied in this lesson. Complete the assessment on another sheet of paper. Be sure to be accurate, but be as creative as you wish!

Food Chain Comic Strip Rubric

Reading the Rubric: Your project has been graded on five criteria. You earned a score from 1 to 5 for each item. Your project is worth a total of 25 points.

Criteria	Poor	Needs Work	Fair	Strong	Excellent
You completely addressed one ecosystem's food chain.	1	2	3	4	5
You demonstrated understanding of food chains.	1	2	3	4	5
You included key facts and vocabulary terms.	1	2	3	4	5
Your work is creative and original.	1	2	3	4	5
Your work is neat and careful.	1	2	3	4	5
Score	____/ 25				
Teacher Comments:					

Social Studies

Exploring Entrepreneurship

Differentiation Strategy

 Discovery Learning

Standards

- Students will understand that entrepreneurs are people who use resources to produce innovative goods and services they hope people will buy.

- TESOL: Students will use English to interact in the classroom.

Materials

- lesson resources (pages 132–135)

- dictionaries

- picture cards with vocabulary terms

- Internet

Procedures

Preparation Note: Before the lesson, post copies of the *Camp Sun Fun Flyer* (page 132) around the classroom, or display it for students to see. Make sure all students have a chance to read the flyer. Then, ask them how they would react if they saw that flyer in their neighborhood.

❶ Display *Kalli's Big Idea* activity sheet (page 133) so students can read it. Read the story aloud as students follow along. Answer students' questions about the story and the task that follows.

❷ Next, introduce important economic vocabulary terms. Divide the class into eight heterogeneous groups and assign each group a different vocabulary word listed below. Students need to look up the word's definition in dictionaries and then create actions to demonstrate each word's meaning.

★ **English Language Support**—Create picture cards for the key vocabulary terms.

---

cost of production—*the idea that price is determined by the cost that goes into making the goods or providing the service*

demand—*the need or desire for a good or service*

entrepreneur—*a person who starts and runs a business*

free enterprise—*business that is based on supply and demand*

goods—*items for sale*

profit—*the money earned minus the money spent to run the business*

services—*work sold at a price*

supply—*the amount of goods or services that people can buy*

Exploring Entrepreneurship

3 Place students in small, heterogeneous groups of three to four students. Distribute copies of the *Project Sun Fun* activity sheet (page 134) to students. Have students read the directions. Model for students how you expect them to complete each item. Fill in the chart at the bottom of the activity sheet with sample numbers. Show students how to compute the costs of production and the profits. Be careful not to give students real numbers and items that they can use; only show them how to fill in the chart.

4 Give groups time to work on their projects. Help them find prices for the supplies that Kalli needs by using the Internet or your own background knowledge. Circulate and assist as needed.

5 Ask each group to think of ways for Kalli to reach her customer base without spending a lot of money. Would she post flyers, design a website, or hand out business cards to neighbors? Have each group design a flyer for Kalli's business. The flyer should include the business name, a business logo, details about the products or services that Kalli offers, and Kalli's contact information.

6 When all groups have completed the project, allow time for students to share their business plans.

7 If students finish early, they may complete the Anchor Activity.

Assessment

Use the *Project Sun Fun Reflection* (page 135) to assess students' learning and to provide a self-assessment opportunity for students.

Anchor Activity

Have students write a jingle for Kalli's business. Then, have them write the script of a radio commercial that includes the jingle. They could also record the jingle or perform it for the class.

Name _____

Kalli's Big Idea

Directions: Read the scenario below.

Kalli was walking home from school one spring afternoon. She was lost in a daydream about summer vacation, which was coming up quickly. She imagined lazy days spent riding her bike and swimming at the local pool. She thought about catching fireflies and picking strawberries. She also thought about how summer days can sometimes get long and boring.

As she rounded the corner near her house, a brightly colored flyer snapped her out of her daydream. She stopped to read what it said.

What a great way to spend a week in the middle of the summer! Kalli wanted to go to Camp Sun Fun. She also knew that her parents would not want to spend $50. She had to come up with a plan to earn the money herself.

Kalli ran home and went straight to her room. She had work to do. She would have to start her own business. She took out a notebook and a pen and began brainstorming business ideas. At the top of the page, she wrote *Project Sun Fun*. She started listing every idea that she had for earning $50 by July 6.

What business could Kalli start to earn $50 in six weeks? Write a detailed business plan to help her pay for Camp Sun Fun.

Name _____

Project Sun Fun

Directions: Work with your group to help Kalli make a plan for earning $50 in six weeks to pay for Camp Sun Fun.

1. **The Problem:** What problem does Kalli need help solving?

   _____

   _____

   _____

2. **The Ideas:** Use the space below to list businesses that would help Kalli earn $50 in six weeks.

3. **The Solution:** Which business idea will work best for Kalli? Describe it below.

   _____

   _____

4. **The Plan:** Explain how Kalli will start and run her business. What supplies does she need? Who will be her customers? When will she work? Whose help will she need?

   _____

   _____

   _____

5. **The Numbers:** Complete the chart below to find out how much Kalli's supplies will cost and how much she will earn. If possible, research prices for the supplies she needs. Show your work in the chart.

Cost of Production	Price of Product	Profit

Name _____

Project Sun Fun Reflection

Business Name: _____

Good/Product/Service: _____

Directions: Think about Project Sun Fun. Answer the questions.

1. What was your favorite part of the assignment?

   _____

   _____

   _____

2. What was the most difficult part of the assignment?

   _____

   _____

   _____

3. What have you learned that you would like to share with others?

   _____

   _____

   _____

4. What would you do differently next time?

   _____

   _____

   _____

Directions: Rate your performance using the dollar sign system.

$$$ = Incredible! $$ = Good $ = Fair

5. Did you do your best work? _____

6. Did you follow directions? _____

7. Did you cooperate with others?_____

8. Were your ideas creative and original? _____

Local Government

Differentiation Strategy

Leveled Learning Centers

Standards

- Students will understand the major things governments do in one's school, community, state, and nation.

- TESOL: Students will use appropriate learning strategies to construct and apply academic knowledge.

Materials

- lesson resources (pages 138–141)

- index cards

- books and websites about local government (See page 167.)

- poster board

- scissors

- chart paper and markers

- craft sticks

- box or bags

Procedures

Note: This lesson is best used to extend student understanding of local governments. To be able to work independently at the learning centers, students will need to be familiar with the services that local governments provide. They also need to know basic vocabulary terms such as *appoint, approve, city council members, elect, fire chief, health and social services, mayor,* and *police chief.*

Preparation Note: Before class begins, set up five learning centers in the classroom. Each center should have enough space for four to six students to work. Stock the centers with lined paper, drawing paper, index cards, and books about local government. It would also be helpful for students at every station to have access to a local chamber of commerce website and poster board.

❶ Copy the *Local Government Center Activities* (pages 138–140), cut them out, and post them at each station. Each page contains leveled activities for above-grade-level, on-grade-level, and below-grade-level students.

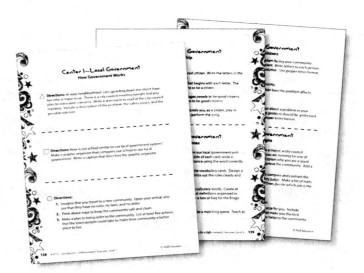

❷ Begin the lesson with a *KWL*-chart activity about local government. On chart paper, make a simple three-column chart. Label the first column *What We Know.* Label the second column *What We Want to Know.* Label the third column *What We Learned.* Work together as a whole class to complete the first two columns. Post the chart in a location where all students can easily see it.

Local Government

3 Explain to students that they will explore five centers to learn more about local government. Have craft sticks marked with triangles, squares, and circles. Distribute the triangle sticks to above-grade-levels students. Distribute the square sticks to on-grade-level students. Distribute the circle sticks to below-grade-level students. Explain that students should choose center activities that match the shapes on their labels.

★ **English Language Support**—Pair English language learners with language-proficient students at the same readiness levels. Give language-proficient students some tips for working with English language learners. Ask them to read the center directions aloud slowly and clearly at least twice. Have them give their partners extra time to respond.

4 Give students time to explore the five centers. Have students choose their own starting points in the rotation. The only limitation is that they must choose a station with an available seat or workspace. Ask students to carefully read the directions. Teach them the "ask three, then me" rule. When following this rule, students must ask three classmates for help before asking the teacher for help. This encourages independence during center activities.

5 If students finish early, they may complete the Anchor Activity.

Assessment

Observe students and ask questions of them as they work at the centers to assess their understanding of the concepts. Use the *Local Government Centers Checklist* (page 141) to document your informal assessment.

Activity Levels
▲
Above Grade Level
■
On Grade Level
●
Below Grade Level

Anchor Activity

Have students create three original activities of varying difficulty for a sixth center about local government. Let students present this new center to the class.

Center 1—Local Government
How Government Works

△ **Directions:** In your neighborhood, cars speeding down the street have become a major issue. There is a city council meeting tonight and you plan to voice your concerns. Write a statement to read at the city council meeting. Include a description of the problem, the safety issues, and the possible solution.

- -

☐ **Directions:** How is our school similar to our local government system? Make a graphic organizer that compares our school to our local government. Write a caption that describes the graphic organizer.

- -

◯ **Directions:**

1. Imagine that you travel to a new community. Upon your arrival, you see that they have no rules, no laws, and no order.

2. Think about ways to keep the community safe and clean.

3. Make a plan to bring order to the community. List at least five actions that the townspeople could take to make their community a better place to live.

Center 2—Local Government
Citizenship

◯ **Directions:**

1. Write an acrostic poem using the word *citizen*. Write the letters in the word down the center of the paper.

2. Think of a word or group of words that begins with each letter. The words should describe what it means to be a citizen.

▢ **Directions:** Create a poster that encourages people to be good citizens. Include one picture and at least five ways to be good citizens.

△ **Directions:** Write a song or rap about the role you, as a citizen, play in government. Ask classmates to help you perform the song.

- -

Center 3—Local Government
Vocabulary Games

Directions: Choose eight vocabulary terms from our local government unit. Make a vocabulary card for each word. On one side of each card, write a vocabulary word. On the other side, write a sentence using the word correctly.

△ **Directions:** Invent an original game using the vocabulary cards. Design a game board to go along with the activity. Write out the rules clearly and simply.

▢ **Directions:** Make a Bingo game using the vocabulary words. Create at least four different boards with the words and definitions organized in different ways. Place the vocabulary cards in a box or bag for the Bingo caller to use during the game.

◯ **Directions:** Use your vocabulary cards to make a matching game. Teach at least one person how to play the game.

Center 4—Local Government
Voice Your Opinions

△ **Directions:** Think about an issue or problem facing your community. Choose two people in your city government. Write letters to each person explaining the problem and a possible solution. Use proper letter format.

◯ **Directions:**

1. Think about a problem in your community.
2. Write a letter to your city mayor. Explain how the problem affects people.
3. Use correct letter format.

▢ **Directions:** Write a letter to your city mayor about a problem in your community. Explain three reasons why the problem should be addressed. Describe a solution to the problem. Use proper letter format.

- -

Center 5—Local Government
Election Campaigns

▢ **Directions:** Think about what it means to be a mayor, a city council member, and a county judge. Imagine that you are running for one of those positions. Write a campaign speech. Explain why you are a good fit for that job and what you plan to do to improve the community. Add a catchy slogan!

△ **Directions:** Use a three-way Venn diagram to compare and contrast the jobs of mayor, city council member, and county judge. Make a list of traits and qualifications needed for each position. Then, decide which job is the best fit for you. Explain your choice.

◯ **Directions:**

1. Imagine that you are a candidate for mayor.
2. Design a sign that will convince people to vote for you. Include a catchy campaign slogan, two qualities that make you the best candidate, and three ideas that you have for helping the community.

Local Government Centers Checklist

Teacher Directions: Use the checklist below to assess students' performance. Use checkmarks (✔) in the criteria columns to indicate proficiency.

Student name	Follows directions and stays on task	Understands function of local government	Understands elements of citizenship	Uses vocabulary related to government	Expresses an opinion on issues related to government	Understands basics of election campaigns

Important Inventions

Differentiation Strategy

 Kaplan's Depth and Complexity

Standards

- Students will understand that technologies often have costs as well as benefits and can have an enormous effect on people and other living things.

- TESOL: Students will use appropriate learning strategies to construct and apply academic knowledge.

Materials

- lesson resources (pages 144–147)
- chart paper and markers
- books, websites, photos and drawings about inventors and inventions *(See page 167.)*
- art supplies
- slide show software
- index cards
- poster board
- scissors
- storage bags

Procedures

Note: This lesson is best used to extend student understanding of important inventions. Students will need to be familiar with a wide variety of inventions and their inventors to successfully answer the questions.

1. Begin the lesson by inviting students to find a partner for a think-pair-share activity. Ask students to discuss the following questions:

   - What is one invention that makes your lives better?

   - What is the most important invention of our time?

   - Do all inventions have a positive impact on the world?

2. Finally, discuss these ideas as a whole class. Record students' ideas on chart paper for use as a reference throughout the lesson.

3. Distribute copies of the *Thinking About Inventions* activity sheets (pages 144–146) to students based on their readiness levels. Have students choose partners who are at their same readiness levels. Partner English language learners with language-proficient students.

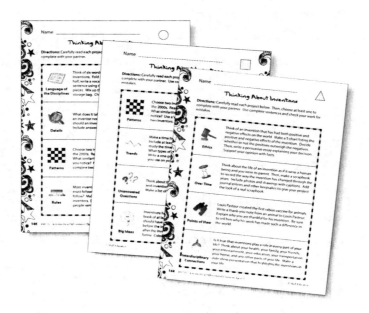

Important Inventions

4 Ask students to carefully read all of the activities on their activity sheets. Read through the *Thinking About Inventions Rubric* (page 147) so that students know how their work will be evaluated. Then, instruct each pair to choose one project to complete.

★ **English Language Support**—Ask students partnered with English language learners to read each item aloud slowly and clearly. Encourage these students to use visual aids, such as photos and drawings from textbooks, picture books, or the Internet to enhance the dialogue.

5 Provide students with the materials needed to help them complete their projects. Give students time to complete their projects. Circulate around the room and assist students as needed.

6 After all students have completed their projects, ask students with the same activity sheets to sit together in a circle. Have each pair of students share their project. Ask students to respond with at least one question and one compliment.

7 If students finish early, they may complete the Anchor Activity.

Assessment

Use the *Thinking About Inventions Rubric* (page 147) to assess students' work.

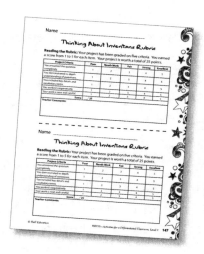

Activity Levels
▲
Above Grade Level
■
On Grade Level
●
Below Grade Level

Anchor Activity

Have students think about three things that they use and enjoy but have no idea who the inventor was. For example, tennis shoes, toothbrushes, climbing walls, or video game systems. Challenge students to research these inventions to find out their origins. Have them create fact cards for each item to display on a bulletin board so that everyone can learn something new.

Name _____

Thinking About Inventions

Directions: Carefully read each project below. Then, choose at least one to complete with your partner. Use complete sentences and check your work for mistakes.

Ethics

Think of an invention that has had both positive and negative effects on the world. Make a T-chart listing the positive and negative effects of the invention. Decide whether or not the positives outweigh the negatives. Then, write a persuasive essay explaining your decision. Support your opinion with facts.

Over Time

Think about the life of an invention as if it were a human being and you were its parent. Then, make a scrapbook to record the way the invention has changed through the years. Include photos and drawings with captions. Add journal entries and other keepsakes to give your project the look of a real scrapbook.

Points of View

Louis Pasteur created the first rabies vaccine for animals. Write a thank-you note from an animal to Louis Pasteur. Explain why you are thankful for his invention. Be sure to tell him why his work has made such a difference in the world.

Interdisciplinary Connections

Is it true that inventions play a role in every part of your life? Think about your health, your family, your friends, your entertainment, your education, your transportation, your home, and any other parts of your life. Make a slide show presentation that highlights the inventions in your life.

Name _____

Thinking About Inventions

Directions: Carefully read each project below. Then, choose at least one to complete with your partner. Use complete sentences and check your work for mistakes.

Patterns

Choose two inventors—one from the 1900s and one from the 2000s. Read about their lives and their inventions. What similarities do you notice? What differences do you notice? Use a Venn diagram to compare and contrast the two inventors.

Trends

Make a time line of major inventions from 1810 to 2010. Include at least 10 inventions on the time line. Then, study the time line carefully. What trends do you see? What types of inventions marked each time period? Write a one-paragraph summary to explain the trends you see on your time line.

Unanswered Questions

Think about the questions you still have about inventors and inventions. Choose one inventor, alive or dead. Make a list of questions you would like to ask that person.

Big Ideas

Inventions have changed our lives in many ways. Create a book of at least five "before and after" comics. Each comic should have only two frames. The first should show life before the invention and the second should show life after the invention. Use exaggeration to make the comics funny. Color the comics and add a cover for the book.

Name _____

Thinking About Inventions

Directions: Carefully read each project below. Then, choose at least one to complete with your partner.

Language of the Disciplines

Think of six words that go along with the topic of inventions. Fold six index cards in half. On the left half, write a vocabulary word. On the right half, write a sentence using the word. Cut the halves apart like puzzle pieces. Mix up the pieces and store them in a plastic storage bag. Challenge friends to play your puzzle game.

Details

What does it take to be an inventor? What skills does an inventor need? What kind of education or training should an inventor have? Write a want ad for an inventor. Include answers to the questions above in your ad.

Patterns

Choose two inventors—one from the 1900s and one from the 2000s. Read about their lives and their inventions. What similarities do you notice? What differences do you notice? Make a two-column "now and then" chart to compare two inventors.

Rules

Most inventors work in laboratories. To stay safe, they must follow basic safety rules. What rules must they follow? Make a poster listing at least five safety rules for inventors. Draw a simple symbol for each rule to help people remember it at a glance.

Name _____

Thinking About Inventions Rubric

Reading the Rubric: Your project has been graded on five criteria. You earned a score from 1 to 5 for each item. Your project is worth a total of 25 points.

Project Criteria	Poor	Needs Work	Fair	Strong	Excellent
You answered the question completely.	1	2	3	4	5
You demonstrated in-depth understanding of inventions.	1	2	3	4	5
You included key details and vocabulary terms.	1	2	3	4	5
You worked cooperatively.	1	2	3	4	5
Your work is neat and careful.	1	2	3	4	5
Score	___/ 25				

Teacher Comments:

- -

Name _____

Thinking About Inventions Rubric

Reading the Rubric: Your project has been graded on five criteria. You earned a score from 1 to 5 for each item. Your project is worth a total of 25 points.

Project Criteria	Poor	Needs Work	Fair	Strong	Excellent
You answered the question completely.	1	2	3	4	5
You demonstrated in-depth understanding of inventions.	1	2	3	4	5
You included key details and vocabulary terms.	1	2	3	4	5
You worked cooperatively.	1	2	3	4	5
Your work is neat and careful.	1	2	3	4	5
Score	___/ 25				

Teacher Comments:

Making Maps

Differentiation Strategy

 Leveled Learning Contracts

Standards

- Students will understand the basic elements of maps and globes.

- TESOL: Students will use English to interact in the classroom.

Materials

- lesson resources (pages 150–153)
- sentence strips
- large map
- sticky tack or tape
- maps of many different types
- poster board
- rulers
- art supplies

Procedures

Preparation Note: Write the terms *compass rose, scale, legend/ key, north, south, east,* and *west* on separate sentence strips. Then, post a large, simple map on the board or on a bulletin board where students can reach it.

★ **English Language Support**—Preteach this vocabulary so students may participate.

❶ Distribute the sentence strips and sticky tack or tape to seven students. One at a time, ask students to place the sentence strips on the map to label the map features. This will provide an opportunity to assess students' background knowledge and to review important vocabulary words.

❷ Display a wide variety of maps around the classroom. Make sure that you include maps of shopping malls, amusement parks, state parks, hotels, and other attractions in addition to the typical world, country, state, and city maps.

❸ Allow students to choose partners for a map exploration. Instruct students to walk around the classroom and study the maps. Ask them to take note of the map features that you reviewed at the beginning of the lesson. Encourage students to appreciate each map's unique qualities. Ask students to choose a favorite map and explain their choices to a partner.

❹ Next, explain to students that they will make a map of a familiar location. Maps must include a title, a compass rose, a legend/ key, and the cardinal directions (north, south, east, and west).

❺ Distribute copies of the *Making Maps Learning Contract* activity sheets (pages 150–152) to students based on their readiness levels. Pair students of the same readiness level for this activity.

Making Maps

6 Ask students with triangle and square sheets to read the directions and fill out their learning contracts. Distribute copies of the *Making Maps Checklist* and *Rubric* (page 153) to students. Clarify any questions that students may have. Meet with students with the circle activity sheets in a small group. Read the directions aloud to them one section at a time, reviewing the checklist and rubric with them.

7 Provide students with necessary materials to help them complete their maps. Have students begin working on their maps. Meet with each pair briefly to review their project plans and sign their learning contracts.

8 As students work, you may want to meet with pairs or small groups of English language learners or below-grade-level students who need extra guidance and support to complete their contract projects.

9 If students finish early, they may complete the Anchor Activity.

Assessment

Remind students to submit their *Making Maps Checklist* and *Rubric* (page 153) with their project. Review students' responses on the checklist portion of the sheet. Then, use the Teacher Rubric portion to assess students' work.

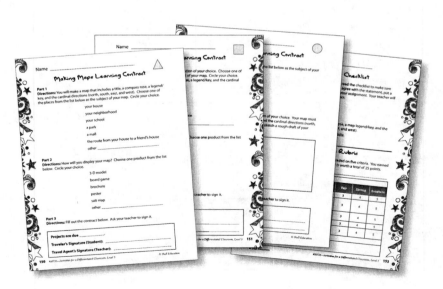

Activity Levels
▲ Above Grade Level
■ On Grade Level
● Below Grade Level

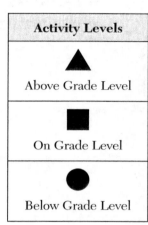

Anchor Activity

Have students choose three locations on their maps. These will be points *A*, *B*, and *C*. Have students use their maps to write directions from one location to the next.

Name _____

Making Maps Learning Contract

Part 1

Directions: You will make a map that includes a title, a compass rose, a legend/key, and the cardinal directions (north, south, east, and west). Choose one of the places from the list below as the subject of your map. Circle your choice.

your house

your neighborhood

your school

a park

a mall

the route from your house to a friend's house

other _____

Part 2

Directions: How will you display your map? Choose one product from the list below. Circle your choice.

3-D model

board game

brochure

poster

salt map

other _____

Part 3

Directions: Fill out the contract below. Ask your teacher to sign it.

Projects are due _____.

Traveler's Signature (Student): _____

Travel Agent's Signature (Teacher): _____

Name _____

Making Maps Learning Contract

Part 1

Directions: You will make a map of the location of your choice. Choose one of the places from the list below as the subject of your map. Circle your choice. Your map must include a title, a compass rose, a legend/key, and the cardinal directions (north, south, east, and west).

> your bedroom
>
> your school
>
> a park
>
> your favorite store
>
> other _____

Part 2

Directions: How will you display your map? Choose one product from the list below.

> 3-D model
>
> board game
>
> brochure
>
> poster
>
> salt map

Part 3

Directions: Fill out the contract below. Ask your teacher to sign it.

Projects are due _____.

Traveler's Signature (Student): _____

Travel Agent's Signature (Teacher): _____

Name _____

Making Maps Learning Contract

Part 1

Directions: Choose one of the places from the list below as the subject of your map. Circle your choice.

classroom

playground

school library

school cafeteria

Part 2

Directions: You will make a map of the location of your choice. Your map must include a title, a compass rose, a legend/key, and the cardinal directions (north, south, east, and west). Use the space below to sketch a rough draft of your map.

Part 3

Directions: Fill out the contract below. Ask your teacher to sign it.

Projects are due _____.

Traveler's Signature (Student): _____

Travel Agent's Signature (Teacher): _____

Name _____

Making Maps Checklist

Directions: Before you turn in your project, read the checklist to make sure you have completed the assignment. If you agree with the statement, put a checkmark (✔) in the box. Turn this in with your assignment. Your teacher will use the bottom half to grade your map project.

Self-Assessment Checklist

Map title: _____

- ❑ My project is complete.
- ❑ My map includes a title, a compass rose, a map legend/key, and the cardinal directions (north, south, east, and west).
- ❑ I showed an understanding of map skills.
- ❑ My map is accurate and easy to read.

Making Maps Rubric

Reading the Rubric: Your project has been graded on five criteria. You earned a score from 1 to 5 for each item. Your project is worth a total of 25 points.

Map title: _____

Name:					
Making Maps Criteria	**Poor**	**Needs Work**	**Fair**	**Strong**	**Excellent**
Your project is complete.	1	2	3	4	5
Your map includes a title, compass rose, legend/key, and cardinal directions.	1	2	3	4	5
You demonstrated map skills.	1	2	3	4	5
You worked cooperatively.	1	2	3	4	5
Your map is accurate and easy to read.	1	2	3	4	5
Score:	___/ 25				
Teacher Comments:					

Cultural Connections

Standards

• Students will understand various aspects of family life, structures, and roles in different cultures and in many eras.

• TESOL: Students will use English to obtain, process, construct, and provide subject matter information in spoken and written form.

Materials

• lesson resources (pages 156–159)

• chart paper and markers

• books about the history of Thanksgiving (See page 167.)

• art supplies

• music and food from different cultures

Procedures

1 Begin the lesson by writing the word *culture* vertically on chart paper. Introduce the meaning of *culture* by writing an acrostic poem using the letters in the word.

Connects us to the past

Unique

Links us to others

Traditions and holidays

Understood by the members of a group

Religion and beliefs

Expressed in food, music, dance, and clothing

2 Explain to students that each person in the room has a culture or more than one culture to which they belong. Help students connect the descriptions in the acrostic poem to examples in their own lives. Provide examples from your own culture to start the discussion. Ask students to tell the class about their traditions, holidays, special foods, and other expressions of their cultures. If many students are eager to discuss the topic, have them think-pair-share so that everyone's ideas are heard.

3 Distribute copies of the *All About My Culture Questionnaire* activity sheet (page 156) to students. Read the questions to students one at a time, pausing between questions for students to provide answers. Some students might need to take this home to be able to fill it out completely. Allow English language learners to draw pictures or explain their answers verbally.

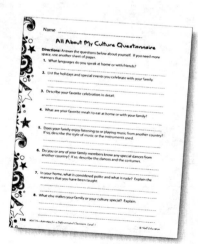

Cultural Connections

❹ Next, distribute copies of the *Exploring My Culture* activity sheets (pages 157–159) to students based on their readiness levels.

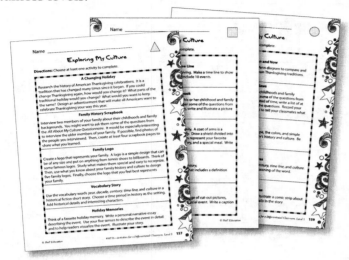

Activity Levels
▲
Above Grade Level
■
On Grade Level
●
Below Grade Level

❺ Instruct students with the triangle and square sheets to carefully read the directions and each activity. Read the directions and the activity choices aloud to students with the circle sheets.

★ **English Language Support**—Read the list of activities aloud to these students. Show examples of the types of projects to make sure that students understand the expectations.

❻ Have students complete at least one activity from the assignment sheets. Circulate and assist as needed.

❼ After all students have completed their projects, hold a class culture celebration to display their work. Ask students to bring in favorite family foods to share. (Have students label ingredients in order to alert any students with food allergies.) Play music that represents the students' cultures. Invite families and other classes to visit the event.

❽ If students finish early, they may complete the Anchor Activity.

Assessment

Evaluate students' work to determine whether the lesson objective was met. You may wish to develop a rubric with students before distributing the assignments.

Anchor Activity

Have students create a wiki or website about their family history and culture. They could include information from the *All About My Culture Questionnaire* activity sheet (page 156) and create links to other websites about their culture or country of origin.

Name _____

All About My Culture Questionnaire

Directions: Answer the questions below about yourself. If you need more space, use another sheet of paper.

1. What languages do you speak at home or with friends?

   _____

2. List the holidays and special events you celebrate with your family.

   _____

   _____

3. Describe your favorite celebration in detail.

   _____

   _____

4. What are your favorite meals to eat at home or with your family?

   _____

   _____

5. Does your family enjoy listening to or playing music from another country? If so, describe the style of music or the instruments used.

   _____

   _____

6. Do you or any of your family members know any special dances from another country? If so, describe the dances and the costumes.

   _____

   _____

7. In your home, what is considered polite and what is rude? Explain the manners that you have been taught.

   _____

   _____

8. What else makes your family or your culture special? Explain.

   _____

   _____

Name _____

Exploring My Culture

Directions: Choose at least one activity to complete.

A Changing Holiday

Research the history of American Thanksgiving celebrations. It is a tradition that has changed many times since it began. If you could change Thanksgiving again, how would you change it? What parts of the traditional holiday would you change? What would you want to keep the same? Design an advertisement that will make all Americans want to celebrate Thanksgiving your way this year.

Family History Scrapbook

Interview two members of your family about their childhoods and family backgrounds. You might want to ask them some of the questions from the *All About My Culture Questionnaire.* It would be especially interesting to interview the older members of your family. If possible, find photos of the people you interviewed. Then, create at least four scrapbook pages to share what you learned.

Family Logo

Create a logo that represents your family. A logo is a simple design that can be of any size and put on anything from tennis shoes to billboards. Think of some famous logos. Study what makes them special and easy to recognize. Then, use what you know about your family history and culture to design five family logos. Finally, choose the logo that you feel best represents your family.

Vocabulary Story

Use the vocabulary words *year, decade, century, time line,* and *culture* in a historical fiction short story. Choose a time period in history as the setting. Add historical details and interesting characters.

Holiday Memories

Think of a favorite holiday memory. Write a personal narrative essay describing the event. Use your five senses to describe the event in detail and to help readers visualize the event. Illustrate your story.

Name _____

Exploring My Culture

Directions: Choose at least one activity to complete.

Thanksgiving Time Line

Research the American tradition of Thanksgiving. Make a time line to show how Thanksgiving has changed over time. Include 10 events.

Personal Storybook

Interview one member of your family about his or her childhood and family background. You might want to ask him or her some of the questions from the *All About My Culture Questionnaire.* Then, write and illustrate a picture book about that person's life.

Family Design

Design a coat of arms that represents your family. A coat of arms is a traditional symbol created to represent a family. Draw a shield divided into four parts. In the four squares, draw symbols to represent your favorite celebration, your family history, a family memory, and a special meal. Write a caption that explains the symbols.

Mini-Dictionary

Look up the vocabulary words *year, decade, century, time line,* and *culture.* Make a mini-dictionary that includes a definition and an illustration for each word.

Holiday Collage

Think of a favorite holiday memory. Make a collage of cut-out pictures, photos, and drawings to tell others about the special event. Write a caption that explains your artwork.

Name _____

Exploring My Culture

Directions: Choose at least one activity to complete.

Thanksgiving Then and Now

Read about the first Thanksgiving. Use a Venn diagram to compare and contrast the first Thanksgiving with your own Thanksgiving traditions.

Family Interviews

Interview two family members about their childhoods and family backgrounds. You might want to ask them some of the questions from the *All About My Culture Questionnaire*. Ahead of time, write a list of at least five questions. Leave space between the questions. Record your relatives' answers in that space. Be prepared to tell your classmates what you learned.

Family Flag

Design a flag for your family. Choose the shape, the colors, and simple symbols that tell something about your family's history and culture. Be prepared to explain your choices.

Vocabulary Pictures

Look up the vocabulary words *year, decade, century, time line,* and *culture*. Draw a picture for each word that shows the meaning of the word.

Comic Strip Memories

Think of a favorite holiday memory. Write and illustrate a comic strip about the event. Include dialogue and interesting details in the story.

Citizenship

Differentiation Strategy

 Menu of Options

Standards

- Students will understand the importance of volunteerism as a characteristic of American society.

- TESOL: Students will use English to obtain, process, construct, and provide subject matter information in spoken and written form.

Materials

- lesson resources (pages 162–165)

- chart paper and markers

- clipboards

- objects, photos, and illustrations that represent memorable citizens from history

- art supplies

Procedures

Preparation Note: Let the school staff and administrators know that your students will be going on a citizenship scavenger hunt. Arrange for small groups of students to observe in the school office, cafeteria, library, and hallways during specific times.

1 Begin the lesson by asking students to explain the meaning of the word *citizenship.* Write their ideas on chart paper. Then, tell students that citizenship is defined as "the way a person behaves toward other people." Write this definition on chart paper.

2 Explain to students that they will be going on a citizenship scavenger hunt. Tell them that they should find and record examples of good citizenship at school. Some examples would be a student picking up trash after lunch, parents volunteering in classrooms, and the principal directing traffic in the parking lot. Distribute clipboards and lined paper to each student. Ask them to take notes about the good citizens that they see.

3 Follow up after the scavenger hunt by having students think-pair-share their observations. Then, invite students to share citizenship examples with the whole class. Add the examples to the chart paper.

4 Discuss the importance of good citizenship. Ask students to think about what the school would be like if there were no good citizens. Then, generalize this to the community, city, state, and country.

5 Distribute copies of the *Citizenship Menu of Options* activity sheets (pages 162–163) to students. Explain to students that they will choose activities from the menu to learn more about citizenship. Decide how many points from the menu that students need to complete. Read the directions and options aloud to students. Set a due date for the projects.

6 Distribute copies of the *Citizenship Plan of Action* activity sheet (page 164) to students. Have students fill out this sheet to plan their projects.

★ **English Language Support**—Work with these students in a small group as they complete the plan of action. This will provide an opportunity to check for understanding and, if necessary, modify activities to meet their needs.

7 Provide students with any needed materials to help them complete the activities. Give students time to complete their activities. Circulate around the room and assist students as needed.

8 If students finish early, they may complete the Anchor Activity.

9 Ask students to choose one of their completed activities to display for a citizenship gallery walk. Then, display the projects and invite families and other students to participate in a gallery walk.

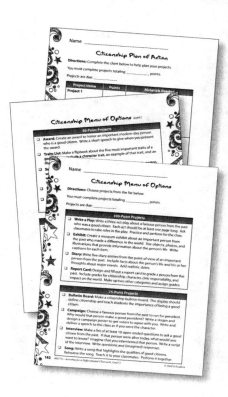

Assessment

Use the *Citizenship Rubrics* (page 165) to assess student work and to provide students with feedback on their projects.

Anchor Activity

Have students interview office staff and other personnel to identify areas of need in the school. Does the custodian need volunteers to pick up trash in the cafeteria after lunch? Does the principal need help monitoring the school halls or restrooms? Does a group of students need reading buddies or mentors? Encourage students to find ways to meet the needs of the school community by being good citizens.

Name _____

Citizenship Menu of Options

Directions: Choose projects from the list below.

You must complete projects totaling _____ points.

Projects are due: _____

100-Point Projects

❑ **Write a Play:** Write a three-act play about a famous person from the past who was a good citizen. Each act should be at least one page long. Ask classmates to take roles in the play. Practice and perform for the class.

❑ **Exhibit:** Create a museum exhibit about an important person from the past who made a difference in the world. Use objects, photos, and illustrations that provide information about the person's life. Write captions for each item.

❑ **Diary:** Write five diary entries from the point of view of an important person from the past. Include facts about the person's life and his or her thoughts about major events. Add realistic dates.

❑ **Report Card:** Design and fill out a report card to grade a person from the past. Include grades for citizenship, character, civic responsibility, and impact on the world. Make up two other categories and assign grades.

75-Point Projects

❑ **Bulletin Board:** Make a citizenship bulletin board. The display should define citizenship and teach students the importance of being a good citizen.

❑ **Campaign:** Choose a famous person from the past to run for president. Why would that person make a good president? Write a slogan and design a campaign poster to get voters to agree with you. Write and deliver a speech to the class as if you were the character.

❑ **Interview:** Make a list of at least 10 open-ended questions to ask a good citizen from the past. If that person were alive today, what would you want to know? Imagine that you interviewed that person. Write a script of the interview. Write questions and (imagined) responses.

❑ **Song:** Write a song that highlights the qualities of good citizens. Rehearse the song. Teach it to your classmates. Perform it together.

Citizenship Menu of Options *(cont.)*

50-Point Projects

❏ **Award:** Create an award to honor an important modern-day person who is a good citizen. Write a short speech to give when you present the award.

❏ **Traits List:** Make a flipbook about the five most important traits of a good citizen. Include a character trait, an example of that trait, and an illustration for each trait.

❏ **Survey:** Take a survey of your neighbors, either by phone or in person, with help from a trusted adult. Ask people for their ideas about what needs to be improved in your neighborhood. Make a T-chart of improvements and possible solutions.

❏ **Time Line:** Make a time line about the life of an important person who showed good citizenship. Include at least 10 events on the time line.

❏ **Venn Diagram:** Make a three-way Venn diagram to compare the definitions of a hero in three different cultures. Research to find out what traits are valued in other cultures.

25-Point Projects

❏ **Compare and Contrast:** Use a Venn diagram to compare two historical figures.

❏ **Poster:** Make a poster of rules for good citizens to follow. Display the poster in the classroom.

❏ **Illustration:** Draw a scene that shows a good citizen in action. Include a caption telling about the picture.

❏ **Question List:** Think of a person you know who is a good citizen. Make a list of 10 questions to ask an outstanding citizen regarding their beliefs.

Name _____

Citizenship Plan of Action

Directions: Complete the chart below to help plan your projects.

You must complete projects totaling _____ points.

Projects are due: _____

Project Name	Points	Materials Needed
Project 1		
Project 2		
Project 3		

Total Points: _____

Citizenship Rubrics

Directions: There are two rubrics below. One rubric is for written projects and the other is for visual projects. Total the amount of points for a final grade.

Writing Project Rubric

Directions: Use this rubric to grade the following projects: *Write a Play, Diary, Report Card, Campaign, Interview, Song, Award, Traits List, Survey, Time Line, Venn Diagram, Compare and Contrast, Poster,* and *Question List.*

Student Name: Total Score: _____ /15	1 = weak 2 = average 3 = strong		
The written project contains appropriate items and information.	1	2	3
The written project is neat and the information is well organized.	1	2	3
The information included in the written project is appropriate to the topic of citizenship.	1	2	3
The written project shows an understanding of the topic of citizenship and its related concepts.	1	2	3
Overall, the final written product represents the student's full potential.	1	2	3

• •

Visual Project Rubric

Directions: Use this rubric to grade the following projects: *Exhibit, Bulletin Board,* and *Illustration.*

Student Name: Total Score: _____ /15	1 = weak 2 = average 3 = strong		
The visual contains appropriate items and information.	1	2	3
The visual is neat and the information is well organized.	1	2	3
The information on the visual is appropriate to the topic of citizenship.	1	2	3
The visual shows an understanding of the topic of citizenship and its related concepts.	1	2	3
Overall, the final visual product represents the student's full potential.	1	2	3

References

Bess, J. 1997. *Teaching well and liking it: Motivating faculty to teach effectively.* Baltimore, MD: The Johns Hopkins University Press.

Brandt, R. 1998. *Powerful learning.* Alexandria, VA: Association for Supervision and Curriculum Development.

Bruner, J. 2004. *Toward a theory of instruction.* Cambridge, MA: Belnap Press of Harvard University Press.

Costa, A. L., and R. Marzano. 1987. Teaching the language of thinking. *Educational Leadership* 45: 29–33.

Gardner, H. 1983. *Frames of mind: The theory of multiple intelligences.* New York: Basic Books.

———. 1999. *Intelligence reframed: Multiple intelligences for the 21st Century.* New York: Basic Books.

Jensen, E. 1998. *Teaching with the brain in mind.* Alexandria, VA: Association for Supervision and Curriculum Development.

Kaplan, S. N. 2001. Layering differentiated curriculum for the gifted and talented. In *Methods and materials for teaching the gifted,* ed. F. Karnes and S. Bean, 133–158. Waco, TX: Prufrock Press.

Olsen, K. D. 1995. *Science continuum of concepts: For grades K–6.* Black Diamond, WA: Books for Educators.

Sprenger, M. 1999. *Learning and memory: The brain in action.* Alexandria, VA: Association for Supervision and Curriculum Development.

Teele, S. 1994. Redesigning the educational system to enable all students to succeed. PhD Diss., University of California, Riverside.

Winebrenner, S. 1992. *Teaching gifted kids in the regular classroom.* Minneapolis, MN: Free Spirit Publishing.

Additional Resources

Where books and websites are referenced in lesson materials lists, some suggestions for these resources are provided below. Shell Education does not control the content of these websites, or guarantee their ongoing availability, or links contained therein. We encourage teachers to preview these websites before directing students to use them.

Page 22—Fairy Tales

http://en.wikipedia.org/wiki/List_of_fairy_tales

Page 28—Nonfiction Text

Darling, Jennifer. *New Junior Cookbook*. Des Moines, IA: Meredith Corporation, 1997.

Harrison, George H. *Backyard Bird Watching for Kids: How to Attract, Feed and Provide Homes for Birds*. Minocqua WI: Willow Creek Press, 1997.

Scholastic Children's Encyclopedia. New York: Scholastic Reference, 2004.

www.make-stuff.com/kids

Page 40—Plot

Hoban, Russell. *A Bargain for Frances*. New York: HarperCollins, 1992.

Penn, Audrey. *Chester Raccoon and the Big Bad Bully*. Terre Haute, IN: Tanglewood Press, 2009.

www.bpl.org/kids/booksmags.htm

www.monroe.lib.in.us/childrens/booklists.html

Page 52—Poetry Skills

Dakos, Kalli. *If You're Not Here, Please Raise Your Hand: Poems about School*. New York: Aladdin Paperbacks, 1995.

Stuart-Clark, Christopher and Michael Harrison. *One Hundred Years of Poetry: For Children*. New York: Oxford University Press, 1999.

Page 64—Rounding and Estimation

Arvoy, Marsha. *Rounding*. New York: Crabtree Publishing Company, 2010.

Dalton, Julie. *Farmer's Market Rounding*. New York: Children's Press, 2007.

Page 106—Earth's Shifting Surface

Lauber, Patricia. *Volcano: The Eruption and Healing of Mt. St. Helens*. New York: Simon & Schuster Children's Publishing, 1993.

Van Rose, Susanna. *Volcanoes and Earthquakes*. New York: DK Children, 2008.

http://video.nationalgeographic.com *(click under Natural Disasters)*

Page 112—Blast Off to Space

http://kids.nineplanets.org

Page 124—Who Swallowed Whom?

Bailey, Jacqui. *Staying Alive: The Story of a Food Chain*. Mankato, MN: Picture Window Books, 2006.

Manning, Mick. *Snap!* London: Frances Lincoln Children's Books, 2006.

www.kids.nationalgeographic.com/kids

Page 136—Local Government

Jakubiak, David J. *What Does a Mayor Do?* New York: PowerKids Press, 2010.

Muschal, Frank. *Local Action*. Ann Arbor, MI: Cherry Lake Publishing, 2007.

www.uschamber.com *(search local chapter)*

Page 142—Important Inventions

Bender, Lionel. *Invention*. New York: DK Children, 2005.

Clements, Gillian. *The Picture History of Great Inventors*. London: Frances Lincoln Children's Books, 2005.

www.uspto.gov

Page 154—Cultural Connections

Colman, Penny. *Thanksgiving: The True Story*. New York: Henry Holt and Co., 2008.

Grace, Catherine O'Neill. *1621: A New Look at Thanksgiving*. New York: National Geographic Children's Books, 2004.

Greenwood, Barbara. *A Pioneer Thanksgiving: A Story of Pioneer Celebrations in 1841*. Tonawanda, NY: Kids Can Press, 1999.

www.history.com/topics/thanksgiving-facts

www.smithsonianmag.com

Contents of the Teacher Resource CD

Lesson Resource Pages

Page	Lesson	Filename
24–27	Fairy Tales	pg024.pdf
30–33	Nonfiction Text	pg030.pdf
36–39	Persuasive Writing	pg036.pdf
42–45	Plot	pg042.pdf
48–51	Life Stories: Biographies and Autobiographies	pg048.pdf
54–57	Poetry Skills	pg054.pdf
60–63	Place Value	pg060.pdf
66–69	Rounding and Estimation	pg066.pdf
72–75	Multiplication Strategies	pg072.pdf
78–81	Playing with Fractions	pg078.pdf
84–87	Finding Perimeter	pg084.pdf
90–93	Symmetry	pg090.pdf
96–99	States of Matter	pg096.pdf
102–105	Forces of Motion	pg102.pdf
108–111	Earth's Shifting Surface	pg108.pdf
114–117	Blast Off to Space	pg114.pdf
120–123	Creature Features	pg120.pdf
126–129	Who Swallowed Whom?	pg126.pdf
132–135	Exploring Entrepreneurship	pg132.pdf
138–141	Local Government	pg138.pdf
144–147	Important Inventions	pg144.pdf
150–153	Making Maps	pg150.pdf
156–159	Cultural Connections	pg156.pdf
162–165	Citizenship	pg162.pdf

Teacher Resources

Title	Filename
Answer Key	answers.pdf
Bingo Board	bingo.pdf
Cause-and-Effect Graphic Organizer	causeeffect.pdf
Comic Strip	comic.pdf
Cube Template	cube.pdf
Hundred Chart	hundred.pdf
One-Inch Graph Paper	graph.pdf
T-Chart	tchart.pdf
Three-Column Chart	threecolumn.pdf
Time Line	timeline.pdf
Triple Venn Diagram	triplevenn.pdf
Venn Diagram	venn.pdf